Vegan Cookbook for Athletes

Meat Free Meals to Fuel Your Workout

Sidney Ellison

© **Copyright 2019 - All rights reserved.**

The contents of this book may not be reproduced, duplicated or transmitted without direct written permission from the author.

Under no circumstances will any legal responsibility or blame be held against the publisher for any reparation, damages, or monetary loss due to the information herein, either directly or indirectly.

Legal Notice:

This book is copyright protected. This is only for personal use. You cannot amend, distribute, sell, use, quote or paraphrase any part or the content within this book without the consent of the author.

Disclaimer Notice:

Please note the information contained within this document is for educational and entertainment purposes only. Every attempt has been made to provide accurate, up to date and reliable complete information. No warranties of any kind are expressed or implied. Readers acknowledge that the author is not engaging in the rendering of legal, financial, medical or professional advice. The content of this book has been derived from various sources. Please consult a licensed professional before attempting any techniques outlined in this book.

By reading this document, the reader agrees that under no circumstances is the author responsible for any losses, direct or indirect, which are incurred as a result of the use of information contained within this document, including, but not limited to, —errors, omissions, or inaccuracies

Books by Sidney Ellison

Scan the Code to Learn More

Plant Based Diet Meal Plan- Delicious Recipes for Clean Eating

Plant Based Diet for Weight Loss- Breakfast Recipes to Melt Fat

Vegan Meal Prep- Zero Worry, Delicious Breakfast Recipes

Vegan Cookbook for Athletes: Lip Smacking Breakfast Recipes for High Performance

Bonus Offer: Get the Ebook absolutely free when you purchase the paperback via Kindle Matchbook!

Table of Contents

Introduction .... - 8 -

Chapter One: An Introduction to the Vegan Diet .... - 9 -

Nutrient-Rich Diet .... - 9 -

Weight Loss .... - 9 -

Improves Kidney Function and Lowers Blood Sugar .... - 10 -

Protection against Some Cancers .... - 10 -

Lower Risk of Heart Disease .... - 11 -

Reduces Pain from Arthritis .... - 11 -

Chapter Two: Vegan Athletic Bread Recipes .... - 14 -

High-Protein Sandwich Bread .... - 14 -

Savory Protein Bread (Vegan, Gluten-Free, Oil-Free) .... - 15 -

Banana Bread .... - 17 -

Seed and Nut Bread .... - 18 -

Healthy Burger Buns .... - 19 -

Chapter Three: Vegan Sauce Recipes .... - 22 -

Mayonnaise .... - 22 -

Tahini Sauce .... - 22 -

Marinara .... - 23 -

Mac n Cheese Sauce .... - 24 -

Vegan Fish Sauce .... - 25 -

Creamy Broccoli Sauce .... - 26 -

Salsa .... - 27 -

Vegan Thai Peanut Sauce...- 27 -

Chapter Four: Pasta Recipes...- 29 -

Mushroom Cream Sauce Pasta...- 29 -

Penne with Black Beans and Vegetables..- 30 -

Tofu Penne Pasta..- 31 -

Spinach Garlic Pasta...- 33 -

Linguine with Guacamole...- 33 -

Lo Mein...- 34 -

Sesame Noodles with Baked Tofu..- 35 -

Chickpea, Spinach & Squash Gnocchi...- 36 -

Dan Dan Noodles with Seitan, Shiitake Mushrooms & Napa Cabbage......................- 37 -

Vegetarian Yakisoba...- 39 -

Chapter Five: Tacos, Burritos and Quesadillas.................................... - 41 -

Tofu Tacos..- 41 -

Quick Bean Tacos...- 42 -

Vegan Enchiladas...- 43 -

Tofu Burritos..- 44 -

Spicy Baked Burritos..- 45 -

Smashed Avocado Vegan Quesadillas...- 47 -

Loaded Vegan Quesadillas...- 48 -

Chapter Six: Casserole Recipes..- 51 -

Moroccan Potato Casserole...- 51 -

Vegetable Moussaka..- 52 -

White Bean Cassoulet .... - 54 -

Zucchini Gratin .... - 55 -

Nutritional values per serving: .... - 55 -

Chapter Seven: Vegan Curries and Stir Fry Recipes .... - 58 -

Green Lentil Curry Masabacha .... - 58 -

Coconut Quinoa Curry .... - 59 -

Chickpea Curry Jacket Sweet Potatoes .... - 60 -

Vegetable and Chickpea Curry .... - 61 -

Tofu Green Bean Stir Fry .... - 62 -

Tofu & Snow Pea Stir-Fry with Peanut Sauce .... - 63 -

Chapter Eight: Vegan Meal Bowl Recipes .... - 65 -

Black Bean-Quinoa Buddha Bowl .... - 65 -

Eggplant and Lentil Bowls .... - 65 -

Asian Tofu & Edamame Bowls .... - 67 -

Tofu Poke Bowl .... - 67 -

Om Buddha Bowl .... - 69 -

Rainbow Buddha Bowl with Cashew Tahini Sauce .... - 70 -

Burrito Buddha Bowl .... - 71 -

One-Pot Burrito Bowl .... - 72 -

Kale Caesar Salad Bowls with Tofu Croutons .... - 74 -

Chapter Nine: Salad Recipes .... - 76 -

Avocado Strawberry Caprese .... - 76 -

Mexican Street Salad .... - 76 -

Mediterranean Bean Salad .... - 77 -

Strawberry Spinach Salad with Avocado & Walnuts .... - 78 -

Apple and Cabbage Slaw .... - 79 -

Black Bean and Corn Salad .... - 79 -

Pineapple & Avocado Salad .... - 80 -

Edamame and Chickpeas Salad .... - 81 -

Black and White Bean Quinoa Salad .... - 82 -

Tempeh "Chicken" Salad .... - 83 -

Edamame Salad .... - 84 -

Chapter Ten: Burgers and Meatballs .... - 85 -

Chickpea Burger .... - 85 -

Black Bean Salsa Burgers with Crispy Potato Rounds .... - 86 -

Three Bean Burger .... - 87 -

Lentil Burgers .... - 88 -

Cauliflower Lentil Burgers .... - 89 -

Lentil "Meatballs" .... - 90 -

Spicy Bean Meatballs .... - 91 -

Quinoa and Black Bean Meatballs .... - 92 -

Chapter Eleven: Vegan Wrap and Sandwich Recipes .... - 95 -

Collard Green Spring Rolls .... - 95 -

Marinated Tempeh Wraps .... - 96 -

Vegan Mediterranean Wraps .... - 97 -

Jackfruit wrap .... - 98 -

Supreme Crunch Wrap.. - 100 -

Bacon and Edamame Wraps... - 101 -

Tempeh Sloppy Joes... - 102 -

BBQ Lentil Sandwich.. - 104 -

Greek Avocado Sandwich... - 105 -

Grilled Nutella Banana Sandwich... - 105 -

Club Sandwich.. - 106 -

Four Layered Sandwich.. - 108 -

Chapter Twelve: Vegan Soup, Stews, and Chili Recipes...................... - 110 -

Spicy Black Bean Soup... - 110 -

Red Curry Quinoa Soup... - 111 -

Split Pea Soup.. - 112 -

Tofu Noodle Soup.. - 113 -

Hot and Sour Soup... - 114 -

Spicy Sun-Dried Tomato Soup with White Beans & Swiss Chard............................. - 115 -

Lentil Spinach Soup.. - 116 -

Potato, Bean and Kale Soup... - 117 -

Healthy Lentil Soup.. - 118 -

Hearty Seitan Stew... - 119 -

Gumbo.. - 120 -

Vegetable Stew... - 122 -

Vegan Chili... - 123 -

Tofu Chili... - 124 -

Easy Vegan Chili Sin Carne...- 125 -

Buffalo Cauliflower Chili..- 127 -

Chapter Thirteen: Rice Recipes...- 128 -

Curried Pumpkin and Mushroom Risotto..- 128 -

Roasted Vegetable and Spinach Risotto...- 129 -

Quick Mexican Brown Rice...- 130 -

Spanish rice..- 131 -

Coconut Rice with Snow Peas..- 132 -

Asian-Style Fried Rice and Beans..- 133 -

Mexican Rice with Black Beans and Corn..- 134 -

Chapter Fourteen: Vegan Mock "Meat" Recipes......................- 136 -

"Liverwurst"..- 136 -

Bolognese...- 137 -

Mushroom Walnut Bolognese..- 139 -

Cashew "Chicken" Stir Fry..- 140 -

Vegan Classic Meatloaf...- 141 -

Lentil Meatloaf...- 143 -

Chickpea "Meat Balls" with Vegetable Marinara Sauce............................- 144 -

Easy BBQ Flavored Baked Tofu..- 147 -

Vegan Mushroom Wellington recipe...- 148 -

Vegan "Chicken" Parmesan..- 149 -

Chapter Fifteen: Vegan Sweet Meal Recipes............................- 152 -

Sweet Potato Pancakes With Cinnamon Maple Sage Butter [Vegan]........- 152 -

    Gluten-free Protein Pancakes .... - 153 -

Chapter Sixteen: Miscellaneous Recipes .... - 155 -

    Simple Vegan Omelet .... - 155 -

    Lentil & Bulgur Pilaf with Green & Yellow Squash .... - 157 -

    Couscous with Chickpeas, Fennel, and Citrus .... - 158 -

    Tomato, Chive, and Chickpea Pancakes .... - 159 -

Chapter Seventeen: Side Dish Recipes .... - 161 -

    Baked Potatoes with Garlic and Rosemary .... - 161 -

    Marinated Mushroom and Eggplant with Peanut Sauce .... - 161 -

    Grilled Brussels sprouts with Balsamic Glaze .... - 163 -

    Izakaya style Japanese Soybeans in a Pod (Edamame) .... - 164 -

    Herbed Corn & Edamame Succotash .... - 165 -

    Stuffed Sweet Potato with Hummus Dressing .... - 166 -

Conclusion .... - 167 -

Introduction

It is difficult to count the number of people who are completely vegan, but there are many people across the globe that are vegetarian. It is estimated that there are over 430 million vegetarians across the globe, and at least 10 million of those vegetarians are vegan, and the number is rapidly growing every year.

People are doing their best to change their fast consumption lifestyle, and one way to change that is becoming vegan. Veganism is not just an ethical choice for the lives of the animals; it is also an eco-friendly choice. Our planet is dying rapidly, and it will take a lot of effort for damage control. But like they say every small step helps, so you can do your bit by turning to veganism. The meat industry or livestock farming as it is called has a huge adverse impact on the environment. It contributes to about 18% of the greenhouse gases, which is a huge number. Turning vegan can definitely help lighten that burden and accelerate our growth towards damage control.

It is not only for this reason that people switch to a vegan lifestyle. There are numerous benefits to the vegan diet, which are explained in detail in the first chapter of the book. There is a strong misconception that the vegan diet lacks substantial protein, and hence it is not ideal for athletes and bodybuilder. Well, in all honesty, it is nothing but a misconception. Athletes can switch to a vegan diet; they just need to identify healthier substitutes for the animal protein, and there are plenty of options.

Over the course of the book, you will learn about the vegan diet and numerous delicious recipes for you to switch to the vegan diet. Use locally sourced ingredients that are easily available in local farmers markets or superstores, so you don't have to worry about finding them.

So without any further ado, let us get started. I hope you enjoy the recipes in the book. Good luck

Chapter One: An Introduction to the Vegan Diet

Most people choose to follow a vegan diet for ethical reasons. The vegan diet, however, offers numerous other health benefits. You can maintain a healthy heart by eating a plant-based diet. The diet also helps to increase your immunity and decreases the risk of developing certain types of cancers and Type II Diabetes. Let us look at six additional benefits of the vegan diet.

Nutrient-Rich Diet

If you are someone who consumes a Western diet, you will need to give up animal products and meat when you switch to a vegan diet. This will mean that you will begin to depend on plant-based foods. If you choose to follow a vegan diet where you consume only whole foods, you will replace the meat and animal products with fruit, whole grains, beans, vegetables, peas, pulses, nuts, and seeds. The consumption of these foods leads to an increase in overall nutrients. For example, studies show that a vegan diet increases your intake of fiber, increases the antioxidants in your body, and intake of beneficial plant compounds. The food that you consume on this diet is rich in folate, magnesium, Vitamins A and C and potassium. That being said, you should understand that not every vegan diet provides the same nutrition.

For example, if you do not plan your diet well, you will consume fewer nutrients like calcium, zinc, iodine, Vitamin B2, fatty acids, and iron. It is for this reason that you should always stay away from those vegan food options that are processed and lack nutrients. Try to base your diet around nutrient-rich fortified and whole plant foods. You can also consider some supplements for essential vitamins like Vitamins B12 and D. Make sure to speak to a medical professional before starting any supplements.

Weight Loss

Numerous people have switched to a vegan diet because this diet is low on processed food and far, which in turn leads to weight loss. Numerous observational studies show that a person following a vegan diet has a lower body mass index and is thinner when compared to non-vegans. In addition to these studies, several controlled studies also reported that a vegan diet is more effective for weight loss when compared to other diets. One study showed that a vegan diet helped the subjects lose at least 9.5 lbs within eighteen weeks. A study was also conducted to understand the effects of a low-calorie diet and a vegan diet on weight. The researchers concluded that people following the vegan diet lost more weight when compared to those who followed a low-calorie diet.

Improves Kidney Function and Lowers Blood Sugar

A vegan diet helps to reduce the risk of developing Type II Diabetes and improve the function of the kidneys. A person following a vegan diet has lower blood sugar, thereby reducing the risk of developing Type II Diabetes by 70%. A study was conducted to understand how the vegan diet helped to reduce blood sugar levels in a diabetic when compared to the diets developed by the American Heart Association (AHA), National Cholesterol Education Program (NCEP) and American Diabetes Association (ADA). It was noted that the vegan diet had a better impact on the blood sugar levels when compared to the other diets. Another study conducted showed that 43% of the participants who followed a vegan diet were able to reduce their blood sugar levels 26% more than the people who were following an ADA-recommended diet. Other studies show that diabetics who swap their Western diet for a vegan diet reduces the risk of poor kidney function.

Protection against Some Cancers

The World Health Organization claims that you can prevent at least one-third of all cancers by controlling different parts of your lifestyle, especially the diet. For instance, you can reduce the risk of developing colorectal cancer by at least ten percent if you consume legumes. Research suggests that you can reduce the risk of cancer by 15% if you consume at least seven portions of vegetables and fresh fruit each week. Vegans often consume a large quantity of fruit, vegetables, and legumes when compared to non-vegans. 96 different studies concluded that the vegan diet could help to reduce developing or dying from cancer by 15%. A vegan diet is rich in soy products, and this can help to reduce the probability of developing breast cancer. When you avoid certain animal products, you can reduce the risk of developing colon, prostate, and breast cancer. A vegan diet helps to reduce the probability of developing cancer because the diet is devoid of processed meat, smoked meat, meat cooked at high temperature and more. These foods are believed to promote the development of specific types of cancer.

People following the vegan diet also avoid the consumption of dairy products. Some studies show that the consumption of dairy products can slightly increase the risk of developing prostate cancer. On the other hand, there is sufficient evidence to prove that the consumption of dairy products can help to reduce the risk of developing cancers like colorectal cancer. Therefore, one cannot say with certainty that the lack of dairy products helps to reduce the risk of developing cancer. It is important that you understand that the studies being referred to in this chapter are only observational. It is difficult to understand why a vegan has a lower risk of developing cancer. Regardless of what the truth may be, it is a good idea to focus on consuming vegetables, fruit and legumes, and reduce your intake of processed, overcooked, and smoked meat.

Lower Risk of Heart Disease

Experts suggest that people should consume legumes, fiber, fruit, and vegetables to decrease the risk of developing heart diseases. When you plan your vegan diet well, you consume these foods in large quantities. Studies that compare the vegan diet and vegetarian diet state that vegans have at least a 75% lower risk of developing hypertension or high blood pressure. A vegan also has a 42% lower risk of dying from heart disease. Numerous controlled studies stated that a vegan diet is more effective at reducing the levels of LDL cholesterol, total cholesterol, and blood sugar when compared to various other diets. This partially helps to improve heart health since any reduction in cholesterol, blood sugar, and blood pressure reduces the risk of developing heart diseases. A vegan, when compared to the general population, consume more nuts and whole grains. These are very good for the heart.

Reduces Pain from Arthritis

Some studies have reported that a vegan diet has a positive effect on people who suffer from arthritis. A study was conducted on 40 people who suffered from arthritis. Some were asked to continue to follow their regular diets while the others were asked to follow the vegan diet. The people on the vegan diet were able to function better and had higher energy levels when compared to those who did not change their diets. A few other studies were conducted to understand the effects of raw, fresh, and probiotic-rich vegan diet on the symptoms of arthritis. These studies reported that people following the vegan diet experienced reduced pain, morning stiffness, and joint swelling.

In simple words, a vegan diet can provide a wide array of health benefits. Researchers and nutritionists are still not sure why these benefits occur. There is, however, no harm in increasing your intake of whole, nutrient-rich, and plant food in your diet.

It is hard for people to switch to a different diet for many reasons. They are used to consuming specific types of food, and if they quit consuming those foods at once, they will begin to have withdrawal symptoms. Your body is used to specific types of food, and it will crave for that food which will make it hard for you to stick to the diet. Instead of going cold turkey, you should try to swap the food you usually consume with the food that you can consume when you follow the vegan diet. Here are a few tips:

1. Make vegetables the star of your meal. Try to consume a small salad for every meal. Make sure that there are more vegetables on your plate than any other type of food.
2. When you are hungry, eat a fruit or a bowl of nuts and seeds. This will help you overcome any cravings that you may have.
3. Keep yourself hydrated.

Most people make the mistake of giving the word 'diet' a negative connotation. It is for this reason that most of them are unable to stick to a diet when they want to switch to a different lifestyle. It is important that you do not do that. Tell yourself that you are switching to a healthier lifestyle that has numerous benefits. Remember that it is okay to give yourself one cheat meal. You can consume this meal on those days when you have cravings. You should remember to never make a habit out of it. Once you begin to lead a vegan lifestyle fully, you will no longer have any meat cravings.

Now that you have learned the benefits of switching to a vegan lifestyle, and understand that there are ample plant-based or nut-based proteins that can help you provide your body with the necessary protein and other nutrients, it is time for you to get started with the recipes. The following chapters are a perfect amalgamation of Vegan recipes for bread, burgers, rice, chilies and stews, savory and sweet meals, etc.

So read on and make the switch to a vegan lifestyle.

Chapter Two: Vegan Athletic Bread Recipes

Tip: If the yeast mixture does not become frothy, discard the mixture and make it again. This is for all the bread recipes that contain yeast. The temperature of the warm water should be 110° F. If it is more or lesser, you will not get the right yeast and may end up discarding the mixture.

You can check out my other books for some more bread recipes: Plant-based lunch and Dinner recipes, Plant-based meal plan recipes and Plant-based Meal Prep recipes

High-Protein Sandwich Bread

Number of servings: 15

Nutritional values per serving: 1 slice

Calories – 61, Fat – 1 g, Carbohydrate – 9 g, Fiber – 1 g, Protein – 4 g

Ingredients:

- 2 teaspoons active dry yeast
- ½ cup warm soymilk or any other nondairy milk of your choice
- 1 tablespoon vegetable oil
- ½ tablespoon salt
- 1 ¼ cups whole wheat flour
- ½ cup vital wheat gluten flour
- ½ cup + 2 tablespoons warm water
- 1 tablespoon maple syrup

Directions:

1. Add ½ cup warm water and yeast into a bowl and stir. Set aside for 5 minutes or until lots of tiny bubbles are formed, sort of frothy.
2. Add remaining water, soymilk, salt and maple syrup into another bowl and stir.
3. Pour into the bowl of yeast mixture.

4. Add vital wheat gluten flour and mix with the dough attachment set on low speed. You can also use your hands if you are comfortable with it. I just hate using my hands for making dough. That's one thing I simply hate.
5. Next, add whole-wheat flour and knead into dough. Knead for some more time until soft and shiny, sort of elastic.
6. Grease a bowl generously with some oil and place the dough in the bowl. Turn the dough around in the bowl so that it is greased from all the sides. Cover the bowl with a kitchen towel and place in a warm area for 2 hours or until it doubles in size.
7. Place the dough on your countertop and punch it down. Place it back in the bowl and cover again. Set aside for an hour.
8. Grease a loaf pan with some oil. Also, dust it with some flour.
9. Shape the dough into an oval and place it in the loaf pan. Fold the seams beneath the dough.
10. Bake in a preheated oven at 450° F for 10 minutes.
11. Lower the temperature to 350° F and continue baking for 30-40 minutes or until light brown. It should also sound hollow when tapped.
12. If you want a soft crust, wrap the bread with a slightly moist kitchen towel. If you want a crunchy crust, bake until golden brown and place on a wire rack.
13. Cool for 30 minutes.
14. Cut into 15 slices.
15. Store in a breadbox at room temperature. It can last for 3-4 days.

Savory Protein Bread (Vegan, Gluten-Free, Oil-Free)

Number of servings: 2 loaves (10 slices each)

Nutritional values per serving: 1 slice

Calories – 200, Fat – 11.9 g, Carbohydrate – 16.8 g, Fiber – 5.8 g, Protein – 11 g

Ingredients:

For dry ingredients:

- ½ cup ground flaxseeds
- 1 cup chickpea flour
- 1 teaspoon baking soda
- 4 teaspoons baking powder
- 1 teaspoon salt
- 1 ½ cups quinoa flour
- ½ cup nutritional yeast
- 4 tablespoons dried parsley

For wet ingredients:

- 1 cup tahini
- 2 cups water
- 1 cup cashew yogurt, unsweetened
- 2 tablespoons apple cider vinegar

For topping: (optional)

- Nutritional yeast
- Hemp hearts

Directions:

1. Add all the dry ingredients into a bowl and stir.
2. Add all the wet ingredients into a mixing bowl and whisk well.
3. Add the dry ingredients into the bowl of wet ingredients and mix well.
4. Take 2 loaf pans and line with parchment paper.
5. Divide the batter among the loaf pans. Scatter hemp hearts and nutritional yeast if using.
6. Bake in a preheated oven at 375° F for about 45 minutes or until golden brown on top.
7. Remove from the oven and place on the cooling rack. After about 30 minutes, remove the bread from the pan and cut each into 10 slices.
8. Transfer into a breadbox once cooled. It can last for 3-4 days at room temperature.

Banana Bread

Number of servings: 2 loaves (8 slices each)

Nutritional values per serving: 1 slice without optional ingredients

Calories – 112, Fat – 1.6 g, Carbohydrate – 13 g, Fiber – 5 g, Protein – 12 g

Ingredients:

- 6.3 ounces vegan protein powder
- ½ cup stevia erythritol blend (optional)
- 2 teaspoons baking soda
- 2 cups mashed banana
- 1 cup almond milk, unsweetened
- 1 cup coconut flour
- 4 tablespoons VitaFiber powder
- 1 teaspoon ground cinnamon (optional)
- 1 cup plain non-dairy yogurt
- 1 teaspoon vanilla extract (optional)

Optional ingredients:

- 1 cup berries or chocolate chips or grated carrots etc.

Directions:

1. Add all the dry ingredients into a bowl and whisk well.
2. Add all the wet ingredients into a mixing bowl and whisk well.
3. Add the dry ingredients into the bowl of wet ingredients and mix well. Your batter will be very thick. Add the optional ingredients if using and stir.
4. Take 2 loaf pans and line with parchment paper.
5. Divide the batter among the loaf pans.
6. Bake in a preheated oven at 375° F for about 45 minutes or until golden brown on top.
7. Remove from the oven and place on the cooling rack. After about 30 minutes, remove the bread from the pan and cut each into 8 slices.

8. Transfer into a breadbox once cooled. Place in the refrigerator. It can last for 3-4 days. You can also freeze for a month.

Tip: Use overripe bananas for great results. When I have overripe bananas, I generally make this bread. I add some walnuts at times. My kids love this bread in their lunch box.

Seed and Nut Bread

Number of servings: 8

Nutritional values per serving: 1

Calories – 194, Fat – 17 g, Carbohydrate – 6 g, Fiber – 3 g, Protein – 6 g

Ingredients:

- 2 tablespoons whole almonds
- ¼ cup pumpkin seeds
- 1 ½ tablespoons sesame seeds
- 2 tablespoons whole hazelnuts
- 2 tablespoons flax seeds
- ¾ cup almond flour
- 1 tablespoon coconut flour
- ¼ cup hazelnut meal
- ¾ teaspoon baking soda
- ¼ teaspoon salt
- 6 tablespoons cashew or almond milk
- 1 ½ flax eggs
- ½ tablespoon agave nectar
- ½ tablespoon apple cider vinegar
- 3 tablespoons melted coconut oil, cooled

Directions:

1. Add hazelnuts and almonds into the food processor bowl and give short pulses until coarse in texture.
2. Add all the seeds and give short pulses until it is powdered.
3. Add rest of the dry ingredients and give short pulses until well incorporated.
4. Add all the wet ingredients into another bowl and whisk well. Transfer into the food processor and pulse until well incorporated.
5. Let the batter rest for 5 minutes.
6. Place a sheet of parchment paper in a small loaf pan. You can use disposable loaf pans as well.
7. Spoon the batter into the loaf pan.
8. Sprinkle some seeds (that are used in this recipe) on top if desired.
9. Bake in a preheated oven at 350° F for about 30-40 minutes or until golden brown on top.
10. Remove from the oven and place on the cooling rack. After about 30 minutes, remove the bread from the pan and cut into 8 slices.
11. Transfer into a breadbox once cooled. It can last for 3-4 days at room temperature.

Tip: To make 1 flax egg, mix together 1 tablespoon ground flaxseeds and 3 tablespoons water in a bowl. Place in the refrigerator for 15 minutes, it will become thick. If hazelnut flour is unavailable, add the extra almond flour.

Healthy Burger Buns

Number of servings: 4

Nutritional values per serving:

Calories – 159, Fat – 6 g, Carbohydrate – 20 g, Fiber – 2 g, Protein – 4 g

Ingredients:

- 6 tablespoons bread flour
- ½ teaspoon vital wheat gluten (optional)
- ½ tablespoon raw sugar or maple syrup or agave nectar
- 3 tablespoons whole wheat flour

- ¾ tablespoon hot cereal mix
- ¾ teaspoon quick rise yeast
- 1 tablespoon virgin olive oil
- ¼ teaspoon salt or to taste
- ¼ teaspoon dried basil flakes
- 1/3 cup water
- ½ tablespoon vegan butter
- ½ teaspoon lemon juice

Directions:

1. Add ¼ cup water into a saucepan. Place saucepan over medium heat. When it begins to boil, add hot cereal and simmer until tender.
2. Turn off the heat and allow it to cool until warm.
3. Stir in yeast and sugar. Let it rest for 10 minutes until frothy.
4. Add rest of the ingredients and stir until well incorporated and dough is formed.
5. If the dough is too hard, add a little water, a tablespoon at a time and knead into a smooth and soft dough. You should knead for at least 4 to 5 minutes. You can use your hands or the mixer for kneading.
6. Place the dough in a bowl. Cover with a cloth and set aside for about an hour. The dough would have risen by now.
7. Divide the dough into 4 equal portions and shape into buns. Place on a baking sheet lined with parchment paper. Leave some gap between the buns.
8. Spray the top of the buns with water. Top with sesame seeds if desired. Next spray some cooking spray over the buns. Cover the baking sheet with a kitchen towel and set aside in a warm area for 40-50 minutes or until it doubles in size.
12. Uncover and bake in a preheated oven at 350° F for about 15-20 minutes.
16. Remove from the oven and place on the cooling rack. . It should also sound hollow when tapped.
9. Remove the baking sheet from the oven and spray some water on top of the buns. Now spray some cooking spray on top of the buns.
10. Place on the cooling rack to cool completely.

Tip: You can use garlic flakes instead of dried basil. You can also add some freshly crushed pepper.

Chapter Three: Vegan Sauce Recipes

Mayonnaise

Makes: 4 cups

Nutritional values per serving: 1 tablespoon

Calories – 62, Fat – 6.9 g, Carbohydrate – 0.2 g, Fiber – NA, Protein – 0.1 g

Ingredients:

- 2 cups unrefined sunflower oil
- 4 teaspoons apple cider vinegar
- 1 cup soymilk, unsweetened
- Sea salt to taste

Directions:

1. Add soymilk, salt, and vinegar in a blender and blend until smooth.
2. With the blender running on low speed, pour oil in a thin stream, through the feeder tube. Slowly raise the speed to high speed and blend until thick.
3. If the mayonnaise is too thick, dilute with a little more soymilk. If it is watery, then add some more oil and blend.
4. Transfer into an airtight container and refrigerate until use. It can last for 3-4 days.

Tip: Make sure that the milk and oil are at room temperature. If the mayonnaise is very thick, add some more milk. If it is runny, add more oil. You can use any oil of your choice; personally, I prefer olive oil. You could replace apple cider vinegar with lemon juice.

Tahini Sauce

Makes: 4 cups

Nutritional values per serving: 4 tablespoons

Calories – 180, Fat – 15 g, Carbohydrate – 7 g, Fiber – 1 g, Protein – 5 g

Ingredients:

- 6 cloves garlic, minced
- Salt to taste
- 2 cups tahini paste
- ½ cup lemon juice
- 1 ½ cups lukewarm water or more if required
- A handful fresh parsley, minced (optional)

Directions:

1. To make the tahini paste: Place a heavy skillet over medium heat. Add sesame seeds. Stir until golden brown. Keep a watch on the seeds as they can get burnt easily. Turn off the heat and cool completely.
2. Transfer into a food processor. Add about ¼ cup olive oil. Blend until a paste is formed. Add more live oil if the paste is too thick and blend again.
3. Store in an airtight jar in the refrigerator. It can last for many months.
4. Measure out 2 cups of the tahini paste to make tahini sauce.
5. Place garlic and salt in a blender. Add tahini paste, lemon juice, and water. Blend until smooth.
6. Transfer into an airtight container. Add parsley just before using tahini sauce.
7. Refrigerate until use. Can store up to 5 days.

Marinara

Makes: 2 -2 ½ cups

Nutritional values per serving: ½ cup

Calories – 80, Fat – 4 g, Carbohydrate – 10 g, Fiber – 3 g, Protein – 2 g

Ingredients:

- 2 ¼ pounds fresh tomatoes, roughly chopped
- 4 tablespoons extra-virgin olive oil

- 1 small sprig fresh basil
- 3 cloves garlic, minced
- Salt to taste

Directions:

1. Add tomatoes into the food processor bowl. Give short pulses until it is chopped into very small pieces.
2. Place a wide saucepan or skillet over medium heat. Add oil. When the oil is heated, add garlic and sauté until fragrant.
3. Add tomatoes and salt and stir.
4. When it begins to boil, lower the heat and cook. Make a few cuts with a knife, on the sprig of basil and add into the sauce. Do not cover while cooking.
5. Stir occasionally and cook until thickness you desire is achieved.
6. Cool and transfer into an airtight glass container. Refrigerate until use. It can store for 6-7 days.

Mac n Cheese Sauce

Makes: 3 cups

Nutritional values per serving: 6 tablespoons

Calories – 138, Fat – 4 g, Carbohydrate – 18 g, Fiber – 6 g, Protein – 11 g

Ingredients:

- 2 tablespoons Earth balance or any other non-dairy butter substitute
- 2 tablespoons cornstarch or flour or arrowroot powder
- 12 tablespoons nutritional yeast
- 2 cups canned pumpkin
- 2 teaspoons sage or to taste (optional)
- 1 teaspoon ground cinnamon or to taste (optional)
- 1 ½ cups almond milk, unsweetened
- ½ teaspoon garlic powder
- 4 teaspoons Dijon mustard
- Salt to taste
- Pepper to taste

Directions:

1. Place a heavy-bottomed pot over medium-low heat. Add earth balance and allow it melt.
2. Add milk, garlic powder, and cornstarch into a bowl and whisk until well incorporated.
3. Pour the mixture into the pot. Stir constantly. It will thicken in a while.
4. Add pumpkin puree and mix well. Let it simmer for a few minutes until heated thoroughly. Stir constantly to prevent burning.
5. Add Dijon mustard and nutritional yeast. Simmer for a couple of minutes. Turn off the heat. Add salt and pepper and stir. Use with pasta. Cool the leftovers completely.
6. Transfer into an airtight container. Refrigerate until use. It can last for 7 days.

Vegan Fish Sauce

Makes: 1 ½ - 2 cups

Nutritional values per serving: 1 tablespoon

Calories – 22.9, Fat – 0 g, Carbohydrate – 5.37 g, Fiber – NA g, Protein – 0.6 g

Ingredients:

- 1 cup shredded wakame
- 4 large cloves garlic, peeled, crushed
- 2/3 cup mushroom flavored dark soy sauce or regular soy sauce or tamari
- 4 cups filtered water
- 2 teaspoons whole peppercorns
- 2 teaspoons genmai miso (optional)

Directions:

1. Wakames are edible seaweeds. Add water, wakame, peppercorns and garlic into a saucepan. Place the saucepan over medium heat. When it begins to boil, reduce the heat and simmer for 20-30 minutes.

2. Strain the liquid through a wire mesh strainer, place over a bowl. Pour the strained liquid back into the saucepan.
3. Stir in the soy sauce and simmer until the liquid is reduced to half its original quantity. It will be disgustingly salty to taste.
4. Turn off the heat and add miso if using. Mix well.
5. Transfer into a bottle. Fasten the cap and refrigerate until use. Use this sauce instead of fish sauce if the recipe calls for it.

Creamy Broccoli Sauce

Makes: 2 ½ -3 cups

Nutritional values per serving: 2 tablespoons

Calories – 128, Fat – 10.3 g, Carbohydrate – 6.7 g, Fiber – 1.4 g, Protein – 5.4 g

Ingredients:

- 6 cups broccoli florets
- 2 tablespoons white wine vinegar
- 2 tablespoons olive oil
- ½ teaspoon pepper
- 4 cloves garlic, peeled
- 2/3 cup canned whole coconut milk
- 2 tablespoons nutritional yeast
- 1 teaspoon sea salt
- Water, as required

Directions:

1. Place a pot over medium-high heat. Add 10-12 cups water.
2. When it begins to boil, add garlic, 1 teaspoon salt and broccoli. Cook until tender. Drain and cool for a while.
3. Transfer into a blender. Add rest of the ingredients and blend until smooth.
4. Transfer into an airtight container. Refrigerate until use. It can store for 4-5 days.

Tip: This sauce goes well with pasta, and with cold pasta salads.

Salsa

Number of servings: 5

Nutritional values per serving: ½ cup

Calories – 18, Fat – 0 g, Carbohydrate – 4 g, Fiber – 1 g, Protein – 1 g

Ingredients:

- 2 cups ripe tomatoes, deseeded, finely chopped
- 8 cloves garlic, minced (optional)
- ½ small onion, minced
- 2 tablespoons red-wine vinegar
- ¼ cup chopped fresh cilantro,
- 1 jalapeño, deseeded, minced
- Salt to taste
- Cayenne pepper to taste
- ½ teaspoon cumin powder

Directions:

1. Mix together all the ingredients in a bowl and set aside for a while for the flavors to set in.
2. Cover and chill until use. It can last for 3 days.

Tip: You can add some finely chopped bell pepper or some minced ginger.

Vegan Thai Peanut Sauce

Number of servings: 12

Nutritional values per serving:

Calories – 105, Fat – 6 g, Carbohydrate – 11 g, Fiber – 2 g, Protein – 4 g

Ingredients:

- ½ cup peanut butter
- ¼ cup tamari or soy sauce
- 4 cloves garlic, peeled, minced, crushed
- ½ cup water
- 4 tablespoons lime juice
- 4 tablespoons rice vinegar
- 1 tablespoon hot sauce (optional)

Directions:

1. Add all the ingredients into a blender and blend until it is smooth. Add some more water if it is too thick.
2. Pour into a heavy-bottomed saucepan. Place the saucepan over medium heat. Stir constantly until thick.
3. Transfer into an airtight container. Refrigerate until use. It can store for 4-5 days.

Tip: This sauce goes great with almost everything from pasta and noodles to salads and stir-fries. It tastes good on wraps and sandwiches as well. You can add into curries too.

Chapter Four: Pasta Recipes

Mushroom Cream Sauce Pasta

Number of servings: 4

Nutritional values per serving:

Calories – 998, Fat – 17 g, Carbohydrate – 179 g, Fiber – 14 g, Protein – 34 g

Ingredients:

- 4 tablespoons vegan margarine, divided
- 2 cloves garlic, peeled, minced
- 2 ½ cups soymilk or almond milk, unsweetened
- Juice of a lemon
- Freshly cracked pepper to taste
- Salt to taste
- 24 ounces mushrooms of your choice, sliced
- 2 tablespoons flour
- 2 tablespoons chopped fresh parsley + extra to garnish
- 20 ounces cooked pasta (linguine or fettuccini)
- Red pepper flakes to taste (optional)

Directions:

1. Place a heavy-bottomed pan over medium heat. Add 2 tablespoons margarine. When it melts, add mushrooms and garlic and sauté until soft. Transfer into a bowl and set aside.
2. Place the pan back over heat. Add remaining margarine. When it melts, add flour and constantly stir for about a minute.
3. Pour the milk you are using, whisking simultaneously. Keep stirring until thick.
4. Add the mushrooms, lemon juice, parsley, salt and pepper and heat for 3-4 minutes. Turn off the heat.
5. Divide pasta among 4 plates. Divide the sauce and spoon over the pasta.

6. Sprinkle parsley and red pepper flakes if using. Serve hot.

Tip: This sauce can also be served with cauliflower or tofu steaks or some vegan mock meat.

Penne with Black Beans and Vegetables

Number of servings: 3

Nutritional values per serving:

Calories – 315, Fat – 8 g, Carbohydrate – 50 g, Fiber – 7 g, Protein – 13 g

Ingredients:

- 5 ounces uncooked penne pasta
- ½ cup sliced carrots
- ¼ cup thinly sliced green or red bell pepper
- ¼ cup sliced fresh mushrooms
- ½ cup sliced zucchini
- 2 small cloves garlic, minced
- ½ small onion, thinly sliced
- ½ tablespoon chopped fresh basil, or 2 teaspoons dried basil
- ½ tablespoon chopped fresh oregano or 2 teaspoons dried oregano
- ½ tablespoon chopped fresh thyme, or 2 teaspoons dried thyme
- ½ tablespoon chopped fresh parsley
- 1 tablespoon olive oil, divided
- 1/3 chopped cup tomatoes
- ½ can (from a 15 ounces can) black beans, drained
- 3 tablespoons vegan Parmesan cheese
- Salt to taste
- Pepper to taste

Directions:

1. Follow the instructions on the package and cook the pasta.
2. In the meantime, place a skillet over medium heat. Add half the oil. When the oil is heated, add onions and sauté until translucent.
3. Add rest of the vegetables, pasta, salt, dried herbs, and beans. Toss well.
4. Add tomatoes and toss well.
5. Drizzle the remaining oil and toss well.
6. Garnish with parsley and vegan cheese and serve.

Tofu Penne Pasta

Number of servings: 10

Nutritional values per serving:

Calories – 459, Fat – 13 g, Carbohydrate – 70 g, Fiber – NA g, Protein – 18 g

Ingredients:

For tofu:

- 4 square blocks, tofu, drained, pressed of excess moisture, crumbled into small pieces
- 2 teaspoons ground cumin
- 2 teaspoons garlic powder
- 3 tablespoons oil
- 1 cup soy sauce
- ½ teaspoon pepper
- 3 teaspoons chili powder

For pasta:

- 2 tablespoons canola oil
- 6 cloves garlic, pressed
- 8 teaspoons paprika or to taste
- 8 teaspoons garlic powder
- 8 teaspoons garlic powder
- Cayenne pepper to taste

- 1 cup water
- 12 cups vegetable broth
- 10 cups dried penne pasta
- 2 large onions, diced
- 8 teaspoons dried oregano
- 8 teaspoons dried parsley
- 2 teaspoons salt or to taste
- ½ cup nutritional yeast
- 6 cups plant based milk of your choice, unsweetened
- 2 cans tomato sauce
- 3 cups frozen peas

For garnish: Optional

- Vegan Parmesan cheese
- Red pepper flakes
- Chopped fresh parsley

Directions:

1. Add soy sauce, pepper, cumin, chili powder, oil, and garlic powder into a medium-size bowl. Whisk until well combined.
2. Add in the tofu. Let the tofu be well coated with the mixture.
3. Line a large baking sheet with parchment paper. Transfer the tofu onto the baking sheet. Spread it evenly.
4. Bake in a preheated oven at 400° F for 35-45 minutes or until firm. It will be meat-like in texture. Stir a couple of times while baking.
5. Remove from oven and set aside to cool.
6. Meanwhile, place a large Dutch oven over medium flame. Add oil. When the oil is heated, add onions and sauté until translucent.
7. Add garlic and cook until aromatic.
8. Add spices, herbs, salt, nutritional yeast, broth, milk, and tomato sauce and mix well.
9. When it begins to boil, add penne and cook until al dente. Stir often.
10. Turn off the heat. Add peas and tofu and stir. Let it sit for 10 minutes.

11. Garnish with the suggested garnishing's and serve.

Spinach Garlic Pasta

Number of servings: 4

Nutritional values per serving:

Calories – 188, Fat – 3.4 g, Carbohydrate – 33 g, Fiber – 3.1 g, Protein – 7.4 g

Ingredients:

- ½ package (from 16 ounces package) angel hair pasta
- ½ package (from 10 ounces package) frozen chopped spinach, thawed
- 2 large cloves garlic, minced
- ½ tablespoon olive oil
- Salt to taste
- Pepper to taste

Directions:

1. Follow the directions on the package and cook the pasta.
2. Place a skillet over medium heat. Add oil. When the oil is heated, add garlic and sauté for a few seconds until aromatic.
3. Add rest of the ingredients and toss well.
4. Serve hot.

Tip: You can use any pasta sauce if desired. I like my pasta simple, but my husband loves the pasta to be tossed in some pasta sauce.

Linguine with Guacamole

Number of servings: 4

Nutritional values per serving:

Calories – 450, Fat – 20 g, Carbohydrate – 49 g, Fiber – 13 g, Protein – 11 g

Ingredients:

- 8.1 ounces whole-wheat linguine
- 2 avocadoes, peeled, pitted, mashed
- ½ cup chopped fresh cilantro
- 2 small red chilies, deseeded, finely chopped
- Juice of 2 limes
- Zest of 2 limes, grated
- 4 large ripe tomatoes, finely chopped
- 2 red onions, finely chopped
- Salt to taste

Directions:

1. Follow the directions on the package and cook the pasta.
2. Meanwhile, add rest of the ingredients into a large bowl and stir.
3. Add pasta and toss well.
4. Serve warm or at room temperature. It also tastes great when chilled. Personally, I prefer chilled.

Lo Mein

Number of servings: 4

Nutritional values per serving:

Calories – 139, Fat – 8.6 g, Carbohydrate – 9.4 g, Fiber – 4.5 g, Protein – 7.8 g

Ingredients:

- 2 packages kelp noodles
- 2 cups frozen spinach, chopped
- 1 cup shelled edamame
- ½ cup julienne cut carrots
- ½ cup sliced mushrooms

For the sauce:

- 4 tablespoons tamari or soy sauce
- 1 teaspoon ground ginger
- ½ teaspoon Sriracha sauce
- 2 tablespoons sesame oil
- 1 teaspoon garlic powder

Directions:

1. Soak the kelp noodles in a bowl of water for a while. Drain and set aside.
2. To make the sauce: Place a saucepan over medium-low heat. Add all the ingredients for the sauce into the saucepan and heat. Stir frequently.
3. Add noodles and toss well. Sprinkle some water if desired so that the mixture is not very dry.
4. Cook until the noodles are soft. Remove from heat. Let it remain in the pan for a few minutes. By now the liquid in the pan would have dried.
5. Divide into bowls and serve.

Tip: You can add any vegetables of your choice. I generally add some green beans and peas as well.

Sesame Noodles with Baked Tofu

Number of servings: 8

Nutritional values per serving: 1 ¾ cups

Calories – 458, Fat – 18 g, Carbohydrate – 60 g, Fiber – 7 g, Protein – 18 g

Ingredients:

- 16 ounces buckwheat noodles
- 4 scallions, chopped
- 4 teaspoons minced ginger
- 2 tablespoons minced garlic
- 2 teaspoons brown sugar

- 4 tablespoons hoisin sauce
- 4 cups small broccoli florets
- 6 tablespoons toasted peanuts
- 6 tablespoons toasted dark sesame oil
- 4 tablespoons low sodium soy sauce
- 16 ounces tofu, cubed, baked
- 2 cups sliced yellow or orange bell pepper

Directions:

1. Follow the directions on the package and cook the pasta.
2. Place a saucepan over medium heat. Add oil, ginger, garlic, scallions and brown sugar. When the oil is well heated, turn off the heat.
3. Add soy sauce and hoisin sauce. Transfer into a large bowl.
4. Add the rest of the ingredients, including pasta and toss well.
5. Serve.

Tip: You can find another recipe of sesame noodles in my other book - Plant based meal prep recipes.

Chickpea, Spinach & Squash Gnocchi

Number of servings: 8

Nutritional values per serving: 1 ½ cups

Calories – 485, Fat – 6 g, Carbohydrate – 92 g, Fiber – 9 g, Protein – 15 g

Ingredients:

- 2 pounds frozen or shelf-stable gnocchi
- 4 cups thinly sliced butternut squash (peeled)
- 4 cloves garlic, minced
- 4 tablespoons currants
- ½ teaspoon freshly ground pepper
- 2 cans (15 ounces each) chickpeas, rinsed, drained

- 3 tablespoons extra-virgin olive oil
- 1 cup sliced shallots
- 2 cans (14 ounces each) vegetable broth
- 2 tablespoons chopped fresh sage or 2 teaspoons dried rubbed sage
- 16 cups coarsely chopped fresh spinach
- 4 tablespoons balsamic vinegar
- Salt to taste
- Pepper to taste

Directions:

1. Follow the directions on the package and cook the gnocchi, if using frozen. If using shelf-stable, you need not cook the gnocchi.
2. Place a large nonstick skillet over medium heat. Add 2 tablespoons oil. When the oil is heated, add gnocchi and sauté until light brown. Remove into a bowl.
3. Add 1 tablespoon oil. When the oil is heated, add shallot, squash, and garlic and sauté for a couple of minutes.
4. Add currants, broth, sage, and pepper. When it begins to boil, lower the heat and cook until the vegetables are tender.
5. Stir in spinach, salt, gnocchi, and chickpeas. Cook until spinach wilts. Drizzle balsamic vinegar on top and serve.

Tip: If you like cheese, sprinkle some vegan Parmesan cheese and serve.

Dan Dan Noodles with Seitan, Shiitake Mushrooms & Napa Cabbage

Number of servings: 3

Nutritional values per serving:

Calories – 460, Fat – 19 g, Carbohydrate – 56 g, Fiber – 6 g, Protein – 21 g

Ingredients:

- 6 ounces buckwheat noodles
- 2 scallions, whites, finely chopped and greens coarsely chopped
- 1.5 ounces Napa cabbage, sliced
- 1 ½ tablespoons peanut oil or canola oil, divided
- ¼ teaspoon crushed red pepper
- ¼ cup low sodium vegetable broth
- 1 tablespoon dark soy sauce
- 1 tablespoon soy sauce
- ½ teaspoon raw sugar
- 3 tablespoons coarsely chopped, dry roasted cashews
- 4 ounces water-packed seitan
- 1.5 ounces fresh shiitake mushrooms, discard stems, sliced
- ¾ tablespoon minced ginger
- ¾ tablespoon minced garlic
- 1/8 teaspoon toasted, ground Sichuan peppercorns or regular pepper
- 2 tablespoons Chinese sesame paste
- 1 teaspoon hot chili oil

Directions:

1. Follow the directions on the package and cook the pasta.
2. Dry the seitan by patting with a dry towel. Cut into ½ inch strips.
3. Add cabbage, whites of scallions and mushrooms into a bowl. Toss well and set aside.
4. Place a wok or cast-iron skillet over medium-high heat. Add ½ tablespoon soil. When the oil is heated, add seitan and cook until slightly crisp. Remove onto a plate.
5. Add remaining oil and lower the heat to medium, ginger, garlic, and crushed red pepper and sauté for a few seconds until aromatic.
6. Stir in the cabbage mixture and cook for a couple of minutes until cabbage wilts.
7. Add seitan and pepper and toss well. Turn off the heat.
8. Add noodles and toss well. Divide into serving bowls.

9. Place a small saucepan over medium-high heat. Add broth, soy sauce, chili oil, sugar, dark soy sauce, sugar and sesame paste and stir until sugar dissolves completely and the mixture is hot. Turn off the heat.
10. Drizzle sauce on top and serve.

Tip: You can substitute Chinese sesame paste with tahini.

Vegetarian Yakisoba

Number of servings: 2

Nutritional values per serving:

Calories – 325.5, Fat – 8 g, Carbohydrate – 57.4 g, Fiber – 3.8 g, Protein – 12.2 g

Ingredients:

- 4 ounce soba noodles
- ½ tablespoon vegan Worcestershire sauce
- ¼ tablespoon raw sugar
- ¾ tablespoon vegetable oil
- 1 clove garlic, peeled, minced
- 1 carrot, peeled, julienned
- 2 scallion greens, chopped
- 2 tablespoons soy sauce
- 1 teaspoon sambal oelek or hot chili paste
- 1 teaspoon sesame oil
- 1 small onion, peeled, sliced
- ¼ head cabbage, cored, shredded
- ½ tablespoon sesame seeds, toasted

Directions:

1. Follow the directions on the package and cook the noodles.
2. Mix together soy sauce, Worcestershire sauce, chili paste, and sugar and sesame oil in a small bowl.

3. Place a skillet or wok over medium heat. Add vegetable oil and heat it.
4. When the oil is heated, add onions, garlic, carrots, and cabbage. Sauté for 3-5 minutes,
5. Add soba noodles and soy sauce mixture. Mix and heat thoroughly.
6. To serve, garnish with sesame seeds and scallions.

Chapter Five: Tacos, Burritos and Quesadillas

Tofu Tacos

Number of servings: 3

Nutritional values per serving: 4 tacos

Calories – 196, Fat – 4.4 g, Carbohydrate – 28.6 g, Fiber – 8.2 g, Protein – 14.6 g

Ingredients:

- ½ teaspoon coconut oil
- 2 Roma tomatoes, diced
- ½ can (from a 16 ounces can) white beans, rinsed, drained
- ½ package (from a 12 ounces package) firm tofu, drained, pat dried, cut into small cubes
- ½ package (from a 10 ounces package) frozen bell peppers with onions
- Juice of a lime, divided
- 1 teaspoon chili powder
- 1 teaspoon paprika
- 1 teaspoon adobo seasoning
- 1 teaspoon turmeric powder
- 12 leaves Swiss chard
- ½ tablespoon nutritional yeast
- Salt to taste

Directions:

1. Place a skillet over medium heat. Add oil. When the oil is heated, add bell pepper and onion and sauté for a few minutes until tender.
2. Stir in the tomatoes and mix well.
3. Add tofu after about 3 minutes. Heat thoroughly. Stir in the beans and heat well.

4. Add all the spices and half the lime juice. Mix well and cook for a couple of minutes.
5. Place 4 Swiss chard leaves on each serving plate.
6. Divide the filling among the leaves. Sprinkle nutritional yeast and remaining lime juice on top and serve.

Quick Bean Tacos

Number of servings: 3

Nutritional values per serving: 1 taco without toppings

Calories –421, Fat – 9 g, Carbohydrate – 70 g, Fiber – 11 g, Protein – 15 g

Ingredients:

- 3 warm tortillas
- 1 cup cooked rice
- ½ tablespoon extra-virgin olive oil
- Guacamole, to serve
- 1 can vegetarian refried beans, warmed
- ¼ cup salsa
- Toppings of your choice

Directions:

1. Spread the tortillas on your countertop. Divide the refried beans among the tortillas and spread it all over. Scatter rice over it. Spoon some salsa and toppings of your choice.
2. Fold the tortillas in half.
3. Place in a greased baking dish. Brush oil on top and sides of the tortillas.
4. Bake in a preheated oven at 375° F for about 15 minutes or until slightly crisp.
5. Serve with guacamole.

Tip: Suggested toppings are avocado, onion, corn, tomatoes, etc. In my other book – Plant-based meal prep book, you can find the recipe of refried beans. You can use store-bought ones as well.

Vegan Enchiladas

Number of servings: 6

Nutritional values per serving: Without optional toppings

Calories –345, Fat – 7 g, Carbohydrate – 59 g, Fiber – 9 g, Protein – 11 g

Ingredients:

For enchilada sauce:

- 3 cups tomato sauce
- 2 teaspoons ground cumin
- 2 teaspoons onion powder
- 2 teaspoons garlic powder
- 2 teaspoons Mexican oregano, crushed
- 2 teaspoons chili powder
- 1 cup low sodium vegetable broth

For burritos:

- 2 cups cooked rice
- 1 cup chopped red bell pepper
- 6 gluten-free tortillas
- 2 cups canned spicy black beans or normal black beans
- Salt to taste
- Pepper to taste
- 1 cup shredded vegan cheese

Optional toppings:

- 1 large tomatoes, chopped

- Pickled peppers and onions
- Creamy avocado green sauce
- Salsa
- Guacamole etc.

Directions:

1. To make the enchilada sauce: Add tomato sauce, spices, oregano and broth into a pan. Place the pan over medium heat. When it begins to boil, lower the heat and simmer for 4-5 minutes. Turn off the heat.
2. To make burritos: Add rice, bell pepper, salt, pepper, and black beans into a bowl and stir.
3. Place tortillas on your countertop. Divide the bean mixture among the tortillas.
4. Fold like a burrito.
5. Take a baking dish and spread a thin layer of enchilada sauce on the bottom of the dish.
6. Place the burritos in the dish. Spread remaining enchilada sauce over it. Sprinkle cheese on top.
7. Bake in a preheated oven at 350° F for about 10 minutes and broil for the last 2-3 minutes.
8. Top with the suggested toppings if using and serve.

Tofu Burritos

Number of servings: 2

Nutritional values per serving: Without soy yogurt

Calories – 402, Fat – 21 g, Carbohydrate – 43 g, Fiber – 7 g, Protein – 12 g

Ingredients:

- ½ cup smoked tofu, chopped into tiny cubes
- ½ green bell pepper, deseeded, chopped
- ½ cup canned, chopped tomatoes or 2 tablespoons tomato paste
- 2 tortillas
- ½ onion, chopped

- 1 tablespoon olive oil
- ½ avocado, peeled, pitted, chopped
- Salt to taste
- Pepper to taste
- ½ teaspoon Tabasco or Sriracha sauce
- Soy yogurt, to serve (optional)
- ½ tablespoon chopped cilantro

Directions:

1. Place a skillet over medium-low heat. Add oil. When the oil is heated, add tofu, pepper, and onion and cook for about 10 minutes. Turn off the heat.
2. Add salt, pepper, and tomatoes in a bowl and stir. Add Tabasco sauce if using and stir.
3. Warm the tortillas following the directions on the package.
4. Place tortillas on your countertop. If you are using tomato paste, smear a tablespoon of it on each of the tortillas now.
5. Divide the tofu filling and place along the diameter of the tortillas. If you are using tomatoes, place it over the filling.
6. Fold like a burrito and serve with soy yogurt if using.

Spicy Baked Burritos

Number of servings: 8

Nutritional values per serving:

Calories –396, Fat – 20.9 g, Carbohydrate – 40.4 g, Fiber – 8.7 g, Protein – 17.1 g

Ingredients:

- 2 cups tomato sauce
- 2-3 tablespoons cayenne pepper hot sauce
- 1 teaspoon ancho chili powder
- ½ teaspoon pepper or to taste
- 3 teaspoons ground cumin

- 2 pounds extra-firm tofu, drained, pressed of excess moisture, cut into ½ inch cubes
- ½ cup cilantro
- ½ teaspoon salt or to taste
- 6 cups cauliflower florets
- 4 teaspoons olive oil
- 8 flour tortillas (8 inches each)
- 2 avocadoes, peeled, pitted, sliced
- 2 tablespoons lemon juice
- 4 cloves garlic, peeled, minced
- 4 scallions, chopped

Directions:

1. Add tomato sauce, hot sauce, chili powder, salt, pepper cumin, and cilantro into a bowl and mix until well combined.
2. Place the tofu on a baking sheet lined with parchment paper.
3. Brush the sauce mixture on top of the tofu.
4. Bake in a preheated oven at 400° F for 40 minutes. Flip sides halfway through baking and brush the top of the tofu with some more of the sauce mixture. Remove from the oven and set aside to cool. Transfer into a bowl.
5. Place cauliflower in a bowl. Pour oil and lemon juice over it. Sprinkle garlic and salt and toss well.
6. Transfer onto the baking sheet. Spread it evenly.
7. Bake for 30 minutes. Flip sides halfway through baking.
8. To assemble: Place the tortillas on your countertop. Divide equally the tofu among the tortillas. Next, layer with cauliflower.
9. Scatter some avocado on each tortilla. Drizzle remaining sauce. Sprinkle cilantro and scallions on top.
10. Fold like a burrito and place on a baking sheet.
11. Bake in a preheated oven at 400° F for 10- 15 minutes or until slightly crisp.
12. Serve hot or warm.

Smashed Avocado Vegan Quesadillas

Number of servings: 3

Nutritional values per serving:

Calories – 325, Fat – 14 g, Carbohydrate – 43 g, Fiber – 10 g, Protein – 10 g

Ingredients:

For spice mix:

- ½ teaspoon ground cumin
- 1/8 teaspoon pepper
- 1/8 teaspoon garlic powder
- ½ teaspoon paprika
- 1/8 teaspoon ancho chili powder or any other variety of chili powder
- 1/8 teaspoon salt

For vegetables:

- ½ tablespoon olive oil
- ½ small zucchini or yellow squash, diced
- ½ bell pepper, thinly sliced
- ½ small red onion, thinly sliced

For smashed avocado (guacamole):

- 1 ripe avocado, peeled, pitted mashed
- Salt to taste
- Pepper to taste
- Juice of ½ lime
- ¼ jalapeño, finely chopped

To assemble:

- 3 flour tortillas
- A handful fresh cilantro, chopped

- Salsa, to serve
- ¾ cup vegetarian refried beans
- 2 teaspoons vegetable oil, divided

Directions:

1. Add all the ingredients for spice mix into a bowl and stir.
2. For the vegetables: Place a skillet over medium-high heat. Add oil and heat. Add the vegetables and cook until soft and brown.
3. Stir in the spice mix and stir-fry for a minute or so until aromatic. Turn off the heat.
4. To make mashed avocado: Mix together all the ingredients for mashed avocado in a bowl.
5. To assemble: Place the tortillas on your countertop. Divide the refried beans among the tortillas and spread it on one-half of the tortillas. You can find the recipe of refried beans in my other book- Plant-based meal prep recipes.
6. Next, divide the smashed avocado and place over the refried beans. Your next layer should be of sautéed vegetables. Sprinkle the cilantro on the top. Fold the other half of the tortilla over the filling and press gently.
7. Wipe your skillet and place it over medium heat. Add half the oil and swirl the pan to coat well. You need to cook the quesadillas in batches.
8. Place 1-2 quesadillas in the pan and cook until the underside is golden brown and crisp. Flip sides and cook the other side until golden brown. Similarly, cook the remaining quesadillas.
9. Serve with salsa.

Tip: You can add some vegan cheese. There are great varieties of vegan cheese to choose from.

Loaded Vegan Quesadillas

Number of servings: 3

Nutritional values per serving:

Calories – 114, Fat – 5 g, Carbohydrate – 13 g, Fiber – 4 g, Protein – 4 g

Ingredients:

For fajita vegetables:

- 1 tablespoon coconut oil or avocado oil, divided
- ½ red bell pepper, thinly sliced
- ½ teaspoon chili powder
- Salt to taste
- Pepper to taste
- 1 medium red onion, thinly sliced
- 4 baby Portobello mushrooms, thinly sliced
- ½ teaspoon ground cumin
- ½ can (from a 15.5 ounces can) black beans

To assemble:

- Guacamole – refer the previous recipe
- 3 gluten-free, soft, corn taco tortillas
- Hot sauce (optional)
- ¼ jalapeño, deseeded, thinly sliced (optional)
- Chopped cilantro

Directions:

1. For the vegetables: Place a skillet over medium-high heat. Add ½ the oil and heat. Add onion and sauté until translucent.
2. Stir in the bell pepper and cook until slightly charred.
3. Next, add the mushrooms cook until brown.
4. Stir in the spices and stir-fry for a minute or so until aromatic.
5. Add beans and mix well. Turn off the heat.
6. Place another skillet over medium heat. You can also transfer the vegetables into a bowl. Wipe the skillet and use it again.
7. Add a few drops of the remaining oil. Place a tortilla in the pan. Spread some guacamole on one-half of the tortillas. Spread 1/3 of the vegetables on the guacamole layer.

8. Fold the other half of the tortilla over the filling and press gently.
9. Cook until the underside is golden brown and crisp. Flip sides and cook the other side until golden brown. Similarly, cook the remaining quesadillas.
10. Place the quesadillas on serving plates. Cut into 2 halves.
11. Serve with hot sauce, jalapeño, and cilantro.

Chapter Six: Casserole Recipes

Moroccan Potato Casserole

Number of servings: 12

Nutritional values per serving:

Calories –237, Fat – 12.1 g, Carbohydrate – 30.9 g, Fiber – 5.9 g, Protein – 4.7 g

Ingredients:

For pesto:

- 12 cloves garlic, peeled
- 4 teaspoons paprika
- ½ teaspoon ground cayenne pepper
- Salt to taste
- 1 teaspoon ground cumin
- 1 ½ cups chopped fresh parsley
- 1 ½ cups chopped fresh cilantro
- 6 tablespoons red wine vinegar
- Juice of 2 lemons
- 6 tablespoons olive oil

For potatoes:

- 3 pounds red potatoes, cut into ½ inch thick slices
- 2 yellow bell peppers, cut into 1 ½ inch squares
- 2 large red bell peppers, cut into 1 ½ inch squares
- 3 large green bell peppers, cut into 1 ½ inch squares
- 8 stalks celery, cut into 2 inch pieces
- 4 tablespoons olive oil
- 2 pound tomatoes, cut each into 8 wedges
- Salt to taste

Directions:

1. To make pesto: Add herbs, garlic, and spices into the food processor bowl and process until well combined.
2. Add rest of the ingredients and blend until well incorporated.
3. To make the casserole: Add potatoes, celery, and all the peppers into a bowl. Add pesto and some salt and toss well.
4. Spread into a large shallow baking dish (13 x 9). Use 2 baking dishes if required.
5. Top with tomatoes. Sprinkle oil on top.
6. Cover the dish with foil.
7. Bake in a preheated oven at 350° F for 35 – 40 minutes.
8. Uncover and bake until potatoes are tender.
9. Let it remain in the oven for 15-20 minutes.
10. Serve.

Vegetable Moussaka

Number of servings: 6

Nutritional values per serving:

Calories – 480, Fat – 26 g, Carbohydrate – 46 g, Fiber – 20 g, Protein – 23 g

Ingredients:

For the eggplant layer:

- 4 eggplants, thinly sliced lengthwise into ¼ inch thick slices
- 4 tablespoons olive oil
- 1 tablespoon salt

For the tomato sauce:

- 5 dry textured vegetable protein granules (TVP)
- 2 tablespoons olive oil
- 2 cans (14 ounces each) diced tomatoes

- ½ teaspoon freshly ground pepper
- Salt to taste
- 2 tablespoons soy sauce
- 1 red bell pepper, chopped
- 1 yellow bell pepper, chopped
- 10 cloves garlic, minced
- ½ teaspoon ground nutmeg

For the almond cream:

- 1 cup almonds, soaked in water overnight, peeled
- 2 small cloves garlic, peeled
- 2 teaspoons vinegar
- ¼ teaspoons freshly ground pepper
- 1 cup water
- ¼ teaspoons salt

Directions:

1. Sprinkle salt over the eggplant slices and place in a colander for about 30 minutes.
2. Rinse and squeeze excess moisture from the eggplants.
3. Place a parchment paper on a large baking tray. Place the eggplant slices on it in a single layer. Brush with oil.
4. Bake in a preheated oven at 390° F for about 10 minutes or until golden brown.
5. Remove from the oven and cool.
6. Meanwhile, make the sauce as follows: Place a skillet over medium heat. Add TVP and cover with water.
7. When it begins to boil, cover and cook for 7-8 minutes.
8. Uncover and cook until nearly dry.
9. Add rest of the ingredients of the sauce in it. When it begins to boil, turn off the heat.
10. Lower the heat and simmer for 8-10 minutes.
11. Meanwhile, make the almond cream as follows: Add all the ingredients of almond cream into a blender and blend until smooth.

12. To assemble: Take a baking dish. Place alternate layers of eggplant and tomato sauce with tomato sauce as the last layer.
13. Pour almond cream on top.
14. Bake in a preheated oven at 390° F for about 25-30 minutes.

Tip: If you want a change in taste, replace TVP with an equal amount of mixed, finely chopped nuts. Do not go through steps 6-8.

White Bean Cassoulet

Number of servings: 3

Nutritional values per serving:

Calories – 432, Fat – 10 g, Carbohydrate – 67 g, Fiber – 21 g, Protein – 20 g

Ingredients:

For cassoulet:

- ½ a 15 ounces can diced tomatoes
- 1 stalk celery, chopped
- 2 small leeks, white parts only, sliced
- 1 large carrot, peeled, sliced
- 1 bay leaf
- 1 can (15 ounces each) white beans of your choice, rinsed, drained
- 2 cloves garlic, minced
- 1 cup vegetable stock or water
- ½ tablespoon Italian seasoning
- Salt to taste
- Pepper to taste

For toasted bread crumbs:

- ½ cup coarse breadcrumbs
- ½ teaspoon garlic powder or minced garlic

- 2 tablespoons chopped fresh parsley
- 1 tablespoon olive oil
- Zest of ½ a lemon

Directions:

1. Place a skillet over medium heat. Add about 2-3 tablespoons stock or water. Add leeks and celery and sauté for 3-4 minutes.
2. Add carrots and cook for about 2 minutes. Add garlic and sauté until fragrant.
3. Add rest of the ingredients for cassoulet. Transfer into a baking dish.
4. Bake in a preheated oven at 390º F for about 25-30 minutes.
5. Meanwhile, make the toasted breadcrumbs as follows: Mix together oil, breadcrumbs and garlic and spread on a baking sheet.
6. Bake in a preheated oven at 350º F for about 10 minutes until lightly toasted.
7. Remove from the oven and cool. Add parsley and zest and mix.
8. To serve: Place cassoulet in bowls. Sprinkle toasted breadcrumbs over it and serve.

Zucchini Gratin

Number of servings: 10

Nutritional values per serving:

Calories – 157, Fat – 12 g, Carbohydrate – 8.8 g, Fiber – 2.4 g, Protein – 3.5 g

Ingredients:

For vegan Parmesan:

- 1 ½ cups cashews
- 1 ½ teaspoons salt
- 6 tablespoons nutritional yeast

- ½ teaspoon garlic powder

For gratin:

- 4 medium zucchinis or yellow squash or use 2 of each, cut into thin round slices
- 1 onion, cut into thin rings
- 1 ½ - 2 cups vegan Parmesan cheese
- ½ teaspoon garlic powder
- 2 small bundles asparagus
- Salt to taste
- Pepper to taste
- 5 tablespoons olive oil

Directions:

1. To make vegan Parmesan cheese: Add all the ingredients for vegan Parmesan cheese into a blender and pulse until fine. Do not pulse for long else the cheese will be sticky. Transfer into a bowl. Cover and set aside.
2. Cut about 2-3 inches from the top part of the asparagus and use it in this recipe. Use the remaining part of the asparagus in some other recipe. Cut each piece into 2 halves.
3. Place a cast-iron skillet. Add 1 tablespoon oil. When the oil is heated, add onions and sauté until translucent. Add salt and pepper. Stir and set aside.
4. Add asparagus and zucchinis into a bowl. Add remaining oil, garlic powder, pepper and 4 tablespoons of the prepared vegan Parmesan cheese and toss.
5. Spread the onions all over the pan.
6. Place zucchini in a circular manner, slightly overlapping each other. Place the asparagus pieces at different spots in between the slices of zucchini.
7. Sprinkle remaining cheese on top.
8. Bake in a preheated oven at 400º F for about 30 minutes. Broil for 2-3 minutes.

Tip: If you do not have a cast-iron skillet, you can use any other oven-proof skillet. If you are using zucchini as well as squash, place zucchini and squash alternately at step

Chapter Seven: Vegan Curries and Stir Fry Recipes

Green Lentil Curry Masabacha

Number of servings: 8

Nutritional values per serving: 1 cup lentils, with 2 tablespoons tahini and 1/3 cup vegetables

Calories –402, Fat – 19 g, Carbohydrate – 44 g, Fiber – 8 g, Protein – 17 g

Ingredients:

- 6 tablespoons extra-virgin olive oil
- 3 teaspoons minced garlic
- 1 1/3 cups red lentils, rinsed
- 1 1/3 cups green lentils, rinsed
- 4 cups vegetable broth
- 2 cups water
- 3 teaspoons curry powder
- Salt to taste
- Pepper to taste
- ¼ cup finely chopped red onion
- 1 large onion, finely chopped
- 3-4 cups water, divided
- 2 medium carrots, grated
- 2 cups thinly sliced arugula
- 2 jalapeños, thinly sliced
- 1 ½ cups tahini sauce – refer Chapter: Vegan sauces

Directions:

1. Place a saucepan over medium heat. Add oil. When the oil is heated, add onion and cook until pink. Stir in garlic and sauté for a few seconds until aromatic.
2. Add the lentils, broth, water and curry powder and stir.

3. When it begins to boil. Lower the heat and cover with a lid. Let it simmer for about 20 minutes.
4. Add carrots and some more water if required. Cook until the lentils are very soft and quite disintegrated. Turn off the heat.
5. Add salt and pepper and mix well. Cover and set aside for a few minutes.
6. Divide into bowls. Spoon 2 tablespoons tahini sauce in each bowl.
7. Scatter some arugula, jalapeño, and red onion.
8. Serve.

Coconut Quinoa Curry

Number of servings: 3

Nutritional values per serving: Without rice

Calories – 507, Fat – 32 g, Carbohydrate – 50 g, Fiber – 11 g, Protein – 13 g

Ingredients:

- 1 ½ cups sweet potato cubes
- ½ cup chopped onion
- 1 medium head broccoli, chopped into florets
- ½ can (from a 15 ounces can) chickpeas, drained, rinsed
- 1 can (14.5 ounces) coconut milk
- 14 ounces canned diced tomatoes
- 2 tablespoons quinoa
- ½ tablespoon fresh ginger, grated
- 1 teaspoon tamari sauce
- ½ teaspoon red chili flakes
- ½ teaspoon turmeric powder
- ½ tablespoon garlic, minced
- ½ teaspoon miso or extra tamari
- ½ cup water

Directions:

1. Place a skillet over medium heat. Spray with cooking spray.
2. Add onions and sauté until translucent. Add ginger, garlic and spices, and stir-fry for a few seconds until aromatic.
3. Add rest of the ingredients and stir. Lower the heat and cover with a lid. Cook until the sweet potato is tender and quinoa is cooked.
4. Serve over rice.

Chickpea Curry Jacket Sweet Potatoes

Number of servings: 8

Nutritional values per serving:

Calories – 276, Fat – 9 g, Carbohydrate – 32 g, Fiber – 11 g, Protein – 12 g

Ingredients:

- 8 sweet potatoes
- 3 teaspoons cumin seeds
- 4 cloves garlic, crushed
- 2 green chilies, finely chopped
- 2 inches fresh ginger, peeled, grated
- 2 teaspoons garam masala
- 1 teaspoon turmeric powder
- 2 teaspoons ground coriander
- 4 tablespoons tikka masala paste
- 4 cans (14.5 ounces each) chickpeas
- 4 cans (14.5 ounces each) chopped tomatoes
- Salt to taste
- Lemon wedges to serve
- A handful fresh cilantro, chopped, to garnish

Directions:

1. Pierce the sweet potatoes with a fork all over and place on a baking sheet.
2. Bake in a preheated oven at 400° F for about 30 minutes.

3. Place a large skillet over medium heat. Add oil. When the oil is heated, add cumin seeds. In a few seconds, the seeds will crackle.
4. Stir in the onions and sauté until translucent.
5. Next add ginger, garlic and green chili and sauté for a couple of minutes.
6. Stir in the spices and tikka masala paste and stir for another 2 minutes until nice and aromatic.
7. Add tomatoes and mix well. Lower the heat and simmer for 5 minutes. Add chickpeas and mix well. Continue simmering until curry is thick. Add salt to taste.
8. Remove the sweet potatoes from the oven and split them open lengthwise.
9. Place a sweet potato on each plate. Top with chickpea curry. Sprinkle cilantro and serve with lemon wedges.

Vegetable and Chickpea Curry

Number of servings: 3

Nutritional values per serving: Without quinoa

Calories – 276, Fat – 7.2 g, Carbohydrate – 44.7 g, Fiber – 10.6 g, Protein – 10.9 g

Ingredients:

- 2 teaspoons olive oil
- ½ cup sliced carrots (cut into ¼ inch thick slices)
- ¾ cup chopped onions
- 1 cup peeled, cubed potatoes
- 2 cups cooked chickpeas
- ½ cup green beans, cut into 1 inch pieces
- 1 Serrano chili, deseeded, minced
- ½ a 14.5 ounces can diced tomatoes
- 1 ½ cups fresh baby spinach
- 2 cloves garlic, minced
- ½ teaspoon fresh ginger, peeled, minced
- ½ tablespoon curry powder

- ½ teaspoon salt or to taste
- ½ teaspoon brown sugar
- 2 cups vegetable broth
- ½ cup coconut milk
- ½ teaspoon chili powder
- Lemon wedges to serve

Directions:

1. Place a nonstick pan over medium heat. Add onions and carrots and sauté for a few minutes until translucent.
2. Add ginger and garlic and sauté for a couple of minutes until fragrant.
3. Add rest of the ingredients except coconut milk, spinach, and lemon wedges and stir.
4. Cover and cook until potatoes are fork-tender.
5. Add spinach and coconut milk. Simmer until spinach wilts.
6. Stir and serve over cooked quinoa with lemon wedges.

Tofu Green Bean Stir Fry

Number of servings: 2

Nutritional values per serving:

Calories – 178.5, Fat – 9.6 g, Carbohydrate – 13.75 g, Fiber – 5 g, Protein – 13.5 g

Ingredients:

- 2 cups chopped green beans (stringed, chopped into 1 ½ inch pieces)
- 1 ½ tablespoons extra-virgin olive oil
- 7 ounces tofu, pressed of excess moisture, cut into cubes
- 2 tablespoons vegetable broth or water
- ½ tablespoon maple syrup
- 1 ½ tablespoons tamari sauce or soy sauce
- ½ tablespoon cornstarch
- ¼ teaspoon red pepper flakes

- 1 teaspoon onion powder
- Salt to taste

Directions:

1. Place a wok over medium heat. Add oil. When the oil is heated, add tofu and cook until crisp all over. Remove beans onto a plate.
2. Add beans, tamari sauce and stir. Cover and cook until the beans are crisp as well as tender. Whisk together broth, maple syrup, onion powder and cornstarch in a bowl.
3. Uncover, add salt and red pepper flakes. Increase the heat to high. Cook until the water dries up in the wok. Stir a couple of times while cooking.
4. Add cornstarch mixture and tofu and stir until thick.
5. Serve over rice.

Tofu & Snow Pea Stir-Fry with Peanut Sauce

Number of servings: 2

Nutritional values per serving: 1 ¼ cups stir fry with ½ cup brown rice

Calories – 514, Fat – 27 g, Carbohydrate – 49 g, Fiber – 7 g, Protein – 22 g

Ingredients:

For peanut sauce:

- 3 tablespoons natural peanut butter
- 1 tablespoon soy sauce
- 1 teaspoon hot sauce
- 1 ½ tablespoons rice vinegar
- 1 teaspoon brown sugar

For stir-fry:

- 7 ounces extra-firm or firm tofu, pressed of excess moisture, cut into cubes
- ½ package (from a 14 ounces package) frozen pepper stir-fry vegetables

- 2 cloves garlic, minced
- 1 tablespoon water or more if required
- 1 cup fresh snow peas, trimmed
- 2 tablespoons unsalted, roasted peanuts
- 2 teaspoons canola oil, divided
- 1 tablespoon finely chopped or grated ginger
- 1 cup cooked brown rice

Directions:

1. Add all the ingredients for the sauce into a bowl and whisk until sugar is dissolved completely. You can also use the recipe for Thai peanut sauce in this book in the Chapter- Vegan sauces. That sauce isn't sweetish while this is.
2. Place a nonstick skillet over medium-high heat. Add 1 teaspoon oil. When the oil is heated, add tofu and cook until brown. Remove onto a plate.
3. Add remaining oil into the pan. Add vegetables, garlic and ginger, and stir-fry for about 3 minutes.
4. Add snow peas and water and cover with a lid. Cook until snow peas are crisp as well as tender.
5. Add peanut sauce and tofu and mix well. Heat thoroughly.
6. Serve over rice. Garnish with peanuts and serve.

Tip: Do not thaw the stir-fry vegetables. You can replace tofu with seitan if desired.

Chapter Eight: Vegan Meal Bowl Recipes

Black Bean-Quinoa Buddha Bowl

Number of servings: 2

Nutritional values per serving:

Calories – 500, Fat – 16 g, Carbohydrate – 74 g, Fiber – 20 g, Protein – 20 g

Ingredients:

- 1 ½ cups canned or cooked black beans, rinsed
- ½ cup hummus
- ½ avocado, peeled, pitted, diced
- ¼ cup chopped fresh cilantro
- 1 1/3 cup cooked quinoa
- 2 tablespoons lime juice
- 6 tablespoons Pico de Gallo
- 1 tablespoon water or more if required

Directions:

1. Add beans and quinoa into a bowl and toss well. Divide into 2 bowls.
2. Add hummus, lime juice, and water into a bowl and whisk well.
3. Spoon over the quinoa mixture.
4. Scatter avocado on top. Spoon 3 tablespoons Pico de Gallo on top, in each bowl. Sprinkle cilantro on top.
5. Serve.

Eggplant and Lentil Bowls

Number of servings: 2

Nutritional values per serving:

Calories –518, Fat – 20 g, Carbohydrate – 82 g, Fiber – 17 g, Protein – 14 g

Ingredients:

- 2 tablespoons peanut oil or olive oil, divided
- 1 ¼ teaspoons curry powder, divided
- 1 ¼ teaspoons chili powder, divided or to taste
- 1 medium eggplant (¾ pound), trimmed, cut into 1 inch cubes
- 2 tablespoons prepared salsa
- ¼ teaspoon salt or to taste
- 2 tablespoons lemon or lime juice or to taste
- 2 tablespoons agave nectar or maple syrup
- Freshly ground pepper to taste
- 1 bunch scallions, chopped, set aside a little to garnish
- 1 large ripe mango, peeled, deseeded, diced
- A handful fresh cilantro, chopped
- 2 cups romaine lettuce, torn
- 2 tablespoons chopped roasted peanuts or cashews
- ½ can (from a 15 ounces can) lentils, drained, rinsed or ¾ cup cooked lentils

Directions:

1. Add 1 ½ tablespoons of oil, half the chili powder and half the curry powder into a large bowl. Stir until well combined. Add eggplants into the bowl and stir until the eggplant is well coated with the mixture.
2. Transfer onto a rimmed baking sheet. Spread it in a single layer.
3. Roast in a preheated oven at 500º F for 15-20 minutes or until cooked. Turn the eggplants, half-way through roasting
4. Remove from the oven and let it cool slightly.
5. Add lemon juice, maple syrup or agave nectar, salsa, pepper, salt, remaining oil, remaining chili powder and remaining curry powder into a large bowl.
6. Add eggplant, scallions, and lentils into the bowl. Warm the lentils if desired.
7. Toss until well combined. Taste and adjust the lemon, salt, and pepper if desired.

8. Divide the romaine lettuce among 2 bowls. Divide the lentil mixture and place over the lettuce. Layer with mangoes followed by nuts.
9. Sprinkle cilantro and remaining scallions on top and serve.

Tip: You can serve it chilled. My kids like it chilled, but I like it piping hot.

Asian Tofu & Edamame Bowls

Number of servings: 2

Nutritional values per serving:

Calories –368, Fat – 12 g, Carbohydrate – 44 g, Fiber – 12 g, Protein – 20 g

Ingredients:

- 8 cups spring mix (assorted salad greens)
- 6 ounces baked tofu cubes
- 1 cup edamame
- 2 tablespoons golden raisins
- 4 tablespoons chow mein noodles
- 1 cup shredded cabbage
- 1 cup grated cabbage
- ½ cup mandarin oranges
- 1 cup bamboo shoots (from can)
- 4 tablespoons low sugar Asian sesame vinaigrette (from bottle)

Directions:

1. Add all the ingredients except vinaigrette into a bowl and toss well.
2. Divide into 2 bowls.
3. Drizzle 2 tablespoons vinaigrette in each bowl and serve.

Tofu Poke Bowl

Number of servings: 2

Nutritional values per serving:

Calories – 262, Fat – 15 g, Carbohydrate – 19 g, Fiber – 5 g, Protein – 16 g

Ingredients:

For sauce:

- 2 greens of scallions, thinly sliced
- 2 teaspoons mirin
- ½ tablespoon sesame seeds
- ¼ teaspoon crushed red pepper (optional)
- 2 tablespoons tamari or soy sauce
- 2 teaspoons toasted, dark sesame oil
- 1 teaspoon grated fresh ginger

For tofu poke bowl:

- ½ package (from a 12 ounces package) extra-firm tofu, drained, cut into ½ inch cubes
- 1 tablespoon rice vinegar
- 1 cup pea shoots
- 2 tablespoons chopped, fresh basil
- 2 cups zucchini noodles
- 1 cup shredded carrots
- 2 tablespoons toasted, chopped peanuts

Directions:

1. To make zucchini noodles. Take 1-2 zucchinis and trim the edges. Using a spiralizer, make noodles of the zucchini. You can also use a julienne peeler to make the noodles. Measure out 2 cups and use.
2. Add all the ingredients for the sauce into a bowl and whisk well. Retain 1 tablespoon sauce in a bowl and set aside.
3. Add tofu to the bowl containing remaining sauce. Toss well.
4. Place zucchini in another bowl. Drizzle vinegar over it. Toss well.

5. Divide the zucchini equally into 2 bowls. Divide the tofu and place over the zucchini.
6. Next, layer with equal quantities of carrots and pea shoots.
7. Sprinkle peanuts and basil.
8. Drizzle a half tablespoon of the retained sauce on top, in each bowl and serve.

Om Buddha Bowl

Number of servings: 2

Nutritional values per serving:

Calories – 500, Fat – 25 g, Carbohydrate – 55 g, Fiber – 12 g, Protein – 20 g

Ingredients:

For cauliflower:

- 2 cups cauliflower florets (small florets)
- 1 teaspoon ground cumin
- 2 teaspoons extra-virgin olive oil
- Salt to taste

For dressing:

- 6 tablespoons hot tap water
- 2 tablespoons lemon juice
- 2 teaspoons za'atar
- 1 tablespoon tahini paste
- 2 cloves garlic, minced
- Salt to taste

Other ingredients:

- 3 cups baby kale

- 1 cup cooked or canned chickpeas
- 1 cup cooked quinoa

Directions:

1. To make cauliflower: Add all the ingredients for cauliflower into a baking dish and toss well. Spread it evenly.
2. Roast in a preheated oven at 425° F for about 12 – 15 minutes.
3. To make the dressing: Add all the ingredients for dressing into a bowl and whisk well.
4. To assemble: Divide kale into 2 bowls. Divide equally and layer with – cauliflower and chickpeas.
5. Drizzle as much dressing as required in each bowl and serve.

Tip: 2 teaspoons Za'atar can be replaced with a mixture of 1 teaspoon ground cumin and 1 teaspoon ground coriander.

Rainbow Buddha Bowl with Cashew Tahini Sauce

Number of servings: 2

Nutritional values per serving: with 2 tablespoons sauce

Calories – 361, Fat – 10 g, Carbohydrate – 54 g, Fiber – 14 g, Protein – 17 g

Ingredients:

For cashew sauce:

- 1 ½ cups cashews
- ½ cup packed parsley leaves
- 2 tablespoons extra-virgin olive oil
- Salt to taste
- 1 cup water
- 2 tablespoons lemon juice or apple cider vinegar
- 1 teaspoon tamari or soy sauce

For bowl:

- 1 cup cooked or canned lentils, drained
- 1 cup shredded red cabbage
- ½ cup chopped bell pepper
- ½ cup sliced cucumber
- 1 cup cooked quinoa
- ½ cup grated raw beet
- ½ cup grated carrot
- Toasted, chopped cashews, to garnish (optional)

Directions:

1. To make cashew sauce: Add all the ingredients for the sauce into a blender and blend until smooth.
2. Divide the lentils among 2 bowls. Divide equally and layer in this manner – quinoa, cabbage followed by beet, peppers. Next layer with carrot, cucumber and finally drizzle 2 tablespoons cashew sauce in each bowl. Top cashews if using.

Tip: You can use the remaining cashew sauce in some other recipe, or as a dip or in salads.

Burrito Buddha Bowl

Number of servings: 1

Nutritional values per serving:

Calories – 727, Fat – 55 g, Carbohydrate – 45 g, Fiber – 10 g, Protein – 19 g

Ingredients:

- 4 ounces extra-firm tofu, cut into 1 inch cubes
- ½ tablespoon soy sauce or tamari
- 2 ½ tablespoons + ½ teaspoon extra-virgin olive oil, divided

- ¼ teaspoon chili powder
- 1 small red bell pepper, cut into ½ inch strips
- ¼ avocado, peeled, pitted, chopped
- 1 tablespoon lime juice
- 1 small red onion, cut into ½ inch wedges
- 3 tablespoons water
- ¼ teaspoon ground coriander
- 2 tablespoons packed cilantro leaves + extra to garnish
- ½ cup cooked brown rice
- Salt to taste
- 3 cherry tomatoes, halved
- ¼ cup sliced or torn romaine lettuce
- 1 tablespoon roasted pumpkin seeds

Directions:

1. Place a sheet of parchment paper on a rimmed baking sheet.
2. Add tofu into a bowl. Drizzle ½ tablespoon oil and tamari. Sprinkle chili powder and toss well.
3. Spread it on one part of the prepared baking sheet.
4. Place onion and bell pepper in a bowl. Drizzle ½ teaspoon oil over it. Toss well and place on the other side of the baking sheet.
5. Roast in a preheated oven at 425º F for about 20 minutes or until the vegetables are tender.
6. Meanwhile, add remaining oil, water, avocado, cilantro, coriander, lime juice, and salt into the mini blender jar and blend until smooth.
7. To assemble: Add rice into a serving bowl. Layer with tofu followed by roasted vegetables. Next place lettuce and tomatoes.
8. Drizzle the dressing on top. Garnish with pumpkin seeds and cilantro and serve.

One-Pot Burrito Bowl

Number of servings: 2

Nutritional values per serving: Without toppings

Calories – 389, Fat – 2.8 g, Carbohydrate – 80.5 g, Fiber – NA, Protein – 12.1 g

Ingredients:

- 1 small onion, thinly sliced
- ½ mild red chili, finely chopped
- ½ cup brown rice, rinsed
- ¼ cup water
- ½ teaspoon smoked paprika
- Pepper to taste
- Salt to taste
- ¼ teaspoon ground cumin
- ½ bell pepper of any color, chopped
- ½ can (from a 14.5 ounces can) black beans, drained
- ½ can (from a 14.5 ounces can) chopped tomatoes
- ½ tablespoon hot sauce
- A handful fresh cilantro, chopped to garnish

Optional toppings:

- Sliced spring onions
- Avocado slices
- Guacamole
- Vegan grated cheese
- Salsa etc.

Directions:

1. Add all the ingredients into a pot or Dutch oven and stir. Place the pot over medium heat.
2. Cover and cook until the rice is tender. Stir occasionally. If you find that the rice is uncooked and there is no liquid left in the pot, add some more water.
3. Fluff with a fork and serve in 2 bowls. Garnish with cilantro.
4. Top with optional toppings if using and serve.

Kale Caesar Salad Bowls with Tofu Croutons

Number of servings: 2

Nutritional values per serving:

Calories – 400, Fat – 28 g, Carbohydrate – 19 g, Fiber – 9 g, Protein – 20 g

Ingredients:

For tofu croutons:

- 7 ounces block extra-firm tofu, drained, pressed of excess moisture for about 15 minutes, cut into ¾ inch cubes
- 2 tablespoons vegan Worcestershire sauce
- ½ teaspoon onion powder
- ½ teaspoon garlic powder
- 2 tablespoons lemon juice
- 1 ½ teaspoons olive oil

For salad bowl:

- 4 cups chopped lacinato kale
- 2 tablespoons toasted pumpkin seeds
- ½ avocado, peeled, pitted chopped
- 2 tablespoons nutritional yeast
- ¼ cup bottled vegan Caesar dressing

Directions:

1. Add lemon juice, garlic powder, onion powder, and Worcestershire sauce into a bowl and stir.
2. Add tofu and toss well. Let it marinate for about 15 minutes.
3. Place a skillet over medium heat. Add oil. When the oil is heated, add tofu (without marinade) and cook until golden brown all over.
4. Remove with a slotted spoon and place on a plate lined with paper towels.

5. To assemble: Add kale into a bowl. Sprinkle nutritional yeast over it and toss well.
6. Divide into 2 bowls.
7. Divide the croutons among the bowls. Sprinkle a tablespoon of pumpkin seeds in each bowl.
8. Drizzle dressing on top and serve.

Chapter Nine: Salad Recipes

Avocado Strawberry Caprese

Number of servings: 4

Nutritional values per serving:

Calories – 230, Fat – 15 g, Carbohydrate – 28 g, Fiber – 5 g, Protein – 4 g

Ingredients:

- 2/3 cup balsamic vinegar
- 2 cups grape or cherry tomatoes, halved
- 2/3 cup loosely packed basil leaves, thinly sliced
- 2 cups strawberries, sliced
- 2 medium ripe avocadoes, peeled, pitted, diced
- 3 teaspoons extra-virgin olive oil
- Freshly ground pepper to taste
- Salt to taste
- Toasted sesame seeds or chopped pecans to garnish

Directions:

1. Add vinegar into a small saucepan. Place the saucepan over medium heat.
2. When it begins to boil, lower the heat and simmer until vinegar reduces to half its original quantity. Turn off the heat. Cool completely.
3. Add avocado, tomatoes, and strawberries into a bowl and toss well.
4. Add vinegar and toss well. Add basil, salt, and pepper and toss well.
5. Garnish with sesame seeds or pecans if using and serve.

Mexican Street Salad

Number of servings:

Nutritional values per serving:

Calories – 111, Fat – 6.5 g, Carbohydrate – 9.24 g, Fiber – 4.2 g, Protein – 2.2 g

Ingredients:

- 5 medium radishes, trimmed, finely sliced
- 1 small white cabbage, shredded
- ¼ small red cabbage, shredded
- ¼ cup extra-virgin olive oil
- 4 carrots, peeled, finely sliced
- Handful cilantro, finely chopped
- 4 large jalapeno chilies or to taste, finely sliced
- 2 red onions, peeled, finely sliced
- ½ cup lime juice
- Sea salt to taste

Directions:

1. Add all the ingredients in a bowl except the red cabbage. Toss well.
2. Add the red cabbage just before serving.

Mediterranean Bean Salad

Number of servings: 3

Nutritional values per serving:

Calories – 175, Fat – 4.5 g, Carbohydrate – 26 g, Fiber – 9 g, Protein – 8 g

Ingredients:

- ½ can (from a 15 ounce can) black beans, drained, rinsed
- ½ can (from a 15.5 ounce can chickpeas, drained, rinsed
- 1 clove garlic, peeled, minced
- 2 tablespoons chopped fresh mint
- 2 tablespoons chopped fresh parsley
- ½ cup chopped grape tomatoes

- ¼ cup chopped red onion
- Juice of ½ lemon
- 2 teaspoons olive oil
- Freshly ground pepper to taste
- Kosher salt to taste

Directions:

1. Add olive oil and lemon juice to a small bowl and whisk until emulsified.
2. Add all the rest of the ingredients into a bowl and toss well.
3. Pour dressing over it. Toss well and set aside for 30 minutes at room temperature.
4. Toss again and serve.

Tip: A good idea is to serve over spiralized vegetables like carrots, zucchini, etc.

Strawberry Spinach Salad with Avocado & Walnuts

Number of servings: 2

Nutritional values per serving:

Calories – 296, Fat – 18 g, Carbohydrate – 27 g, Fiber – 10 g, Protein – 8 g

Ingredients:

- 6 cups baby spinach
- 1 cup sliced strawberries
- ½ medium avocado, diced
- 2 tablespoons finely chopped red onion
- 4 tablespoons vinaigrette
- 4 tablespoons toasted walnut pieces

Directions:

1. Add onion, strawberries, and spinach into a bowl and toss well.
2. Pour vinaigrette and toss well.

3. Scatter walnuts and avocado on top and serve.

Apple and Cabbage Slaw

Number of servings: 2-3

Nutritional values per serving: 1 cup

Calories – 98, Fat – 6 g, Carbohydrate – 12 g, Fiber – 3 g, Protein – 1 g

Ingredients:

- 1 cup red cabbage, shredded
- 1 cup green cabbage, shredded
- 1 small Granny Smith apple, discard the stem, chopped
- 1 tablespoon golden balsamic vinegar
- 1 tablespoon olive oil
- 1 teaspoon agave nectar
- ¾ teaspoon poppy seeds
- Freshly ground black pepper to taste
- Kosher salt to taste

Directions:

1. Add olive oil, vinegar, poppy seeds, agave nectar, salt, and pepper into a bowl and whisk well.
2. Add rest of the ingredients into a bowl and toss. Pour dressing over it and fold gently until well combined.
3. Serve as it is or chilled.

Black Bean and Corn Salad

Number of servings: 8

Nutritional values per serving:

Calories – 154, Fat – 1 g, Carbohydrate – 30.9 g, Fiber – 9.8 g, Protein – 7.8 g

Ingredients:

- 2 cans (15 ounces each) black beans, drained, rinsed
- ½ cup red onion, finely chopped
- 1 red bell pepper, chopped
- 1 yellow bell pepper, chopped
- 2 cups fresh corn kernels
- 1 large avocado, peeled, pitted, chopped
- 2 small tomatoes, chopped
- ½ cup fresh cilantro, chopped
- 4 scallions, chopped
- Salt to taste
- Pepper to taste
- Juice of 2 limes
- 2 teaspoons dried basil
- 2 teaspoons dried oregano
- 1 teaspoon ground cumin

Directions:

1. Add all the ingredients into a bowl and toss well.
2. Cover and set aside for a while for the flavors to set in.

Pineapple & Avocado Salad

Number of servings: 4

Nutritional values per serving:

Calories – 186, Fat – 13 g, Carbohydrate – 20 g, Fiber – 5 g, Protein – 2 g

Ingredients:

- 1 medium red onion, sliced into thin rounds
- 1 firm, ripe avocado, peeled, pitted, chopped

- 1 ½ tablespoons extra-virgin olive oil
- ½ tablespoon fresh lime juice
- Freshly ground pepper to taste
- Salt to taste
- 1 small fresh ripe pineapple, skinned, cored, chopped
- Ice water, as required

Directions:

1. Add onions into a bowl of ice water. Let it remain in it for 15 minutes. Drain.
2. To make the dressing: Add oil and lime juice into a bowl. Whisk well.
3. Place the avocado, pineapple, and onions in any manner you desire, on a serving plate. Sprinkle salt.
4. Pour dressing over it. Sprinkle pepper and serve.

Edamame and Chickpeas Salad

Number of servings: 4

Nutritional values per serving:

Calories – 333, Fat – 16.8 g, Carbohydrate – 37.1 g, Fiber – 5.9 g, Protein – 11.5 g

Ingredients:

- 1 cup shelled edamame
- 3 tablespoons minced red onion
- 3 tablespoons minced carrots
- 1 cup cooked chickpeas
- 3 tablespoons minced red bell pepper
- 2 tablespoons dried sweetened cranberries
- 2 tablespoons sunflower seeds
- 3 tablespoons olive oil
- 3 tablespoons apple cider vinegar
- Celery salt to taste
- 3 tablespoons agave nectar
- 1 tablespoon vegan mayonnaise – refer Chapter: Vegan Sauces

- A pinch cayenne pepper or to taste

Directions:

1. Add all of the ingredients into a bowl and toss well.
2. Serve.

Tip: You can substitute mayonnaise with any other dressing of your choice. You can also use flax seeds instead of sunflower seeds.

Black and White Bean Quinoa Salad

Number of servings: 2

Nutritional values per serving:

Calories – 415, Fat – 16 g, Carbohydrate – 55 g, Fiber – NA, Protein – 17 g

Ingredients:

For the salad:

- 3 tablespoons quinoa
- ½ can (from a 15 ounces can) navy beans, drained, rinsed
- ½ can (from a 15 ounces can) black beans, drained, rinsed
- 1 small red onion, chopped
- 1 small cucumber, chopped
- 2 tablespoons chopped fresh cilantro
- 1 small jalapeño, deseeded, chopped (optional)

For the dressing:

- 2 tablespoons vegetable oil
- ½ tablespoon apple cider vinegar
- ¼ teaspoon chili powder
- ¼ teaspoon dried oregano
- Pepper to taste
- Salt to taste

- ½ teaspoon ground coriander
- 1 small clove garlic, minced
- 1 tablespoon lime juice

Directions:

1. To make the dressing: Add all the ingredients of the dressing into a bowl. Whisk well. Set aside for a while for the flavors to set in.
2. Cook quinoa following the instructions on the package but add a bit of salt while cooking. Set aside.
3. Add salad ingredients into a bowl. Add cooked quinoa and toss well.
4. Pour dressing on top. Toss well and serve.

Tempeh "Chicken" Salad

Number of servings: 4

Nutritional values per serving:

Calories – 248.9, Fat – 14.1 g, Carbohydrate – 18 g, Fiber – 1.5 g, Protein – 17.1 g

Ingredients:

- 2 cups tempeh, cubed, steamed, cooled
- 2 sticks celery, chopped
- 1 onion, chopped
- 2 medium pickles, chopped
- ¼ cup parsley, minced
- 1 ½ tablespoons soy sauce
- 1 cup vegan mayonnaise
- 2 cloves garlic minced
- 4 teaspoons mustard
- 3-4 teaspoons curry powder (optional)

Directions:

1. Add all the ingredients to a large bowl. Toss well.

2. Chill for a couple of hours and serve.

Edamame Salad

Number of servings: 4

Nutritional values per serving:

Calories – 240.4, Fat – 8.5 g, Carbohydrate – 35.9 g, Fiber – 6.5 g, Protein – 11.8 g

Ingredients:

- ½ pound frozen edamame, shelled, cooked according to the instructions on the package, drained, rinsed
- ½ red bell pepper, deseeded, chopped
- 1 ½ cups frozen corn kernels
- 1 cup red onions, sliced
- 2 green onions, sliced
- 1 tablespoon chopped fresh oregano or basil
- 2 tablespoons chopped parsley

For dressing:

- 3 tablespoons lemon juice
- 1 tablespoon olive oil
- 1 tablespoon Dijon mustard
- Pepper to taste
- Salt to taste

Directions:

1. To make the dressing: Whisk together all the ingredients of the dressing.
2. Add all of the ingredients to a large bowl and toss well. Pour dressing on top. Toss well. Chill until use.

Chapter Ten: Burgers and Meatballs

Chickpea Burger

Number of servings: 2

Nutritional values per serving: Without serving options

Calories – 161, Fat – 8 g, Carbohydrate – 18 g, Fiber – 3 g, Protein – 6 g

Ingredients:

- ½ can (from a 15 ounces can) chickpeas, rinsed, drained
- ½ small onion, minced
- ½ cup minced fresh parsley
- 2 small cloves garlic, peeled, minced
- ½ teaspoon ground cumin
- ½ teaspoon ground coriander
- 1 tablespoon plain flour
- Salt to taste
- Pepper powder to taste
- 1 tablespoon vegetable oil

To serve:

- ½ cup salsa
- ¼ teaspoon chili powder or harissa paste
- Toasted pita
- Green salad

Directions:

1. Add all the ingredients except oil into the food processor bowl and process until coarse.
2. Divide into 2 equal portions and shape into patties.
3. Place a nonstick skillet over medium heat and add a little of the oil.
4. Place the burgers in the pan and cook on both the sides until golden brown.

5. Stuff the cooked burger in the pita pockets and serve with salsa and a green salad.
6. To make the sauce: Add all the ingredients to a bowl and whisk thoroughly.

Black Bean Salsa Burgers with Crispy Potato Rounds

Number of servings: 2

Nutritional values per serving: 1 bun with a burger and without toppings

Calories – 392, Fat – 6 g, Carbohydrate – 74 g, Fiber – 9 g, Protein – 14 g

Ingredients:

- ½ can (from a 15 ounces can) black beans, rinsed, drained
- ¼ cup brown rice flour
- ½ tablespoon vegetable oil
- ¼ cup old fashioned oats
- 3 tablespoons salsa

To serve:

- 2 burger buns, split
- Sliced avocado
- Lettuce leaves
- Mustard
- Tomato slices etc.

For the potatoes:

- 1 large baking potato, thinly sliced
- ½ teaspoon dried parsley
- ¼ teaspoon paprika
- ¼ teaspoon garlic powder
- ½ teaspoon dried oregano
- Salt to sprinkle

Directions:

1. Place beans in a bowl and mash with a potato masher.
2. Add rest of the ingredients except oil and mix well.
3. If you are not able to form patties from the mixture and it is sort of sticky or runny, add more flour, a teaspoon at a time and mix well each time. If it is too dry, then add salsa, a teaspoon at a time.
4. Divide the mixture into 2 equal portions and shape into patties. Chill for 30 minutes.
5. Place a nonstick skillet over medium heat and add a little of the oil.
6. Place the burgers in the pan and cook on both the sides until golden brown.
7. Serve the burgers in between the buns with suggested toppings or any other toppings of your choice along with crispy potato rounds.
8. Meanwhile, make the crispy potatoes as follows: Line a baking sheet with parchment paper. Grease with cooking spray.
9. Place potatoes in a bowl. Sprinkle all the spices over it and toss well. Spread it evenly on the prepared baking sheet.
10. Roast in a preheated oven at 450º F for about 20 to 30 minutes or until crisp.

Three Bean Burger

Number of servings: 3

Nutritional values per serving:

Calories – 285, Fat – 8 g, Carbohydrate – 39 g, Fiber – 12 g, Protein – 17 g

Ingredients:

- ½ can (from a 15 ounces can) red kidney beans
- ½ can (from a 15 ounces can) cannellini beans
- ½ can (from a 15 ounces can) flageolet beans
- 1 small sweet potato, cooked
- ½ tablespoon poppy seeds
- ½ tablespoon sesame seeds
- 1 heaping tablespoon pea protein

Directions:

1. Add all the ingredients into a bowl and mash with a potato masher.
2. Divide into 2 equal portions and shape into patties.
3. Place a nonstick skillet over medium heat and add a little of the oil.
4. Place the burgers in the pan and cook on both the sides until golden brown.
5. You can also grill the burgers after brushing with oil.
6. Serve over buns or lettuce or wraps if desired etc.

Lentil Burgers

Number of servings: 4

Nutritional values per serving:

Calories – 356, Fat – 12 g, Carbohydrate – 41 g, Fiber – 11 g, Protein – 17 g

Ingredients:

For burgers:

- 1.3 pounds cooked or canned red or brown lentils
- 2 spring onions, finely chopped
- 1 teaspoon sesame seeds
- 3.5 ounces chickpea flour
- Salt to taste
- Vegetable oil, to fry, as required

For slaw:

- 4 courgettes, peeled into thin, long ribbons
- 4 carrots, peeled into thin, long ribbons
- Salt to taste
- 1 teaspoon sesame oil
- 2-3 tablespoons lime juice
- ½ cup chopped fresh cilantro

Directions:

1. For the slaw: Add carrots, courgettes, sesame seeds, cilantro, lime juice, and sesame oil into a bowl and toss well.
2. Add all the ingredients for burger into a bowl and mix well. Mash lightly.
3. Divide the mixture into 8 equal portions and shape into patties.
4. Place a nonstick pan over medium heat. Add a tablespoon of oil. Place a few burgers in the pan. Cook until the underside is golden brown. Flip sides and cook the other side until golden brown.
5. Repeat the previous step and fry the remaining burgers.
6. Remove the patties with a slotted spoon and place on a plate lined with paper towels.
7. Serve with slaw. Serve over burger buns if desired.

Cauliflower Lentil Burgers

Number of servings: 12

Nutritional values per serving: Without buns or toppings

Calories – 148, Fat – 1 g, Carbohydrate – 24 g, Fiber – 10 g, Protein – 13 g

Ingredients:

- 2 cups cooked brown lentils
- 2 cups chopped onions
- 4 tablespoons nutritional yeast
- 2 teaspoons Dijon mustard
- 1 teaspoon ground cumin
- ½ teaspoon chipotle chili
- 6 cups cauliflower rice
- 4 cups chopped bell pepper
- 2 teaspoons minced garlic
- 1 teaspoon smoked paprika
- ½ teaspoon pepper or to taste

For glaze:

- 2 teaspoons liquid smoke
- 2/3 cup unsweetened ketchup

Directions:

1. To make cauliflower rice: Place the cauliflower rice in the food processor bowl. Pulse until you get rice-like texture. You can also grate the cauliflower with a box grater to rice-like texture.
2. Place a skillet over medium heat. Add onion and bell pepper and sauté until slightly soft.
3. Add rest of the ingredients into the food processor and process until just incorporated. It should not be smooth.
4. Transfer into a bowl. Make 12 equal portions of the mixture and shape into patties.
5. Grill on a preheated grill on both the sides until brown.
6. Add ketchup and liquid smoke into a bowl and stir. Spread it over the burgers. Grill for a minute on each side.
7. Serve over buns if desired with toppings of your choice.

Lentil "Meatballs"

Number of servings: 12

Nutritional values per serving: 2 meatballs without pasta or sauce

Calories –48, Fat – 0 g, Carbohydrate – 12 g, Fiber – NA, Protein – 3 g

Ingredients:

- 1 cup dried green lentils, rinsed
- 2 medium yellow onions, chopped
- 8 cloves garlic, minced
- 2 teaspoons ground sage
- 3 cups water
- 1 cup brown rice
- 2 carrots, grated

- 2 teaspoons ground cumin
- 2 teaspoons sea salt
- 2 cups vegetable broth

Directions:

1. Add lentils, onion, cumin, salt, brown rice, carrot, sage, water, broth and garlic into a saucepan.
2. Place the saucepan over medium heat. When the mixture begins to boil, lower the heat and simmer until tender. It may take a couple of hours to cook. Transfer into a colander and drain off the extra liquid from the lentils. Let it sit in the colander for 10 minutes. You can make this in a pressure cooker. It is quicker.
3. Transfer into the food processor bowl and process until a few lentils are visible and most of it is smooth.
4. Divide the mixture into 24 equal portions and shape into balls.
5. Place a nonstick pan over medium heat. Spray some cooking spray. Place a few of the meatballs. Cook until brown all over. Remove onto a plate.
6. Cook the remaining in batches similarly.
7. Serve as it is or over pasta with a sauce of your choice.

Tip: You can bake the meatballs in the oven. Just spray some cooking spray over the meatballs and then bake.

Spicy Bean Meatballs

Number of servings: 4

Nutritional values per serving: 2 meatballs

Calories – 117, Fat – 1 g, Carbohydrate – 22 g, Fiber – 7 g, Protein – 7 g

Ingredients:

- 2 large cloves garlic, crushed
- 4.4 ounces cooked or canned kidney beans, drained, rinsed
- 5.3 ounces cooked or canned chickpeas, drained, rinsed

- ¼ medium apple, grated
- 2 tablespoons chopped fresh parsley
- 3 tablespoons tomato puree
- ½ tablespoon ground coriander
- Chili powder to taste
- ½ teaspoon ground cumin
- White pepper to taste
- ¼ teaspoon turmeric powder
- ¼ teaspoon ground cinnamon
- Salt to taste
- 2 tablespoons brown rice flour

Directions:

1. Add kidney beans, chickpeas, tomato puree, and apple into a mixing bowl. Mash well using a potato masher.
2. Add rest of the ingredients and mix well.
3. Divide the mixture into 8 equal portions and shape into balls.
4. Place a nonstick pan over medium heat. Spray some cooking spray. Place a few of the meatballs. Cook until brown all over. Remove onto a plate.
5. Cook the remaining in batches similarly.
6. Serve as it is or over pasta with a sauce of your choice.

Tip: Try replacing these beans with any other beans of your choice. Each time I make it, I try it out with different beans, and they all taste different.

Quinoa and Black Bean Meatballs

Number of servings: 6

Nutritional values per serving: 1 meatball

Calories – 67.4, Fat – 1.9 g, Carbohydrate – 10 g, Fiber – 2.7 g, Protein – 3.3 g

Ingredients:

For meatballs:

- ½ cup cooked, cooled quinoa
- 1 tablespoon water or olive oil
- ¼ cup diced shallots
- ½ tablespoon fresh oregano or ¼ tablespoon dried oregano
- ¼ teaspoon fennel seeds (optional)
- 1 tablespoon tomato paste
- 1 tablespoon vegan Worcestershire sauce (optional)
- ½ can (from a 15 ounces can) black beans, rinsed, drained, pat dried
- 2 cloves garlic, minced
- 1/8 teaspoon sea salt or to taste
- ¼ teaspoon red pepper flakes
- ¼ cup vegan Parmesan cheese + extra to serve
- 1 tablespoon chopped parsley
- 1 tablespoon chopped basil

To serve:

- Marinara sauce (optional)

Directions:

1. Spread the black beans on a baking sheet lined with parchment paper.
2. Bake in a preheated oven at 350° F for about 20 minutes or until dry and some of them crack. Remove the baking sheet from the oven and let it cool.
3. Place a skillet over medium heat. Add water or oil. When it heats, add garlic and shallot and cook until tender. Turn off the heat.
4. Transfer into the food processor bowl. Also add the beans, oregano, fennel, and red pepper flakes. Process until roughly powdered.
5. Add rest of the ingredients for meatballs and pulse until well combined and sort of like dough. Taste and adjust the seasoning.
6. Scoop out 2 tablespoons of the mixture and shape into balls. Place on a plate. Refrigerate for 15 minutes.
7. Place a nonstick pan over medium heat. Spray some cooking spray. Place a few of the meatballs. Cook until brown all over. Remove onto a plate.

8. Cook the remaining in batches similarly.
9. Serving with marinara sauce is a great idea. You can serve it over pasta.

Chapter Eleven: Vegan Wrap and Sandwich Recipes

Collard Green Spring Rolls

Number of servings: 6

Nutritional values per serving: 1 wrap

Calories – 95, Fat – 5 g, Carbohydrate – 9.7 g, Fiber – 2.6 g, Protein – 6 g

Ingredients:

For spring rolls:

- 5 ounces extra-firm tofu, pressed of excess moisture, cut into cubes
- ½ small red bell pepper, thinly sliced
- ½ cup packed basil
- 3 small carrots, very finely chopped
- 6 collard green leaves, slice off the stems
- ¾ cup bean sprouts
- ½ cup finely sliced red cabbage

For sauce:

- 3 tablespoons unsalted, creamy sunflower seed butter
- 1 tablespoon maple syrup or to taste
- ¼ teaspoon chili garlic sauce
- 1 tablespoon tamari or soy sauce
- 1 tablespoon lime juice
- Hot water, to dilute, as required

Directions:

1. To make the sauce: Add all the ingredients for the sauce into a bowl and whisk until smooth. Taste and adjust the ingredients if required.

2. Place the collard green leaves on your countertop. Divide the tofu, basil, red pepper, carrot, bean sprouts and cabbage among the leaves, along the central line of the leaf.
3. Fold the leaf over the filling. Fold the sides and roll it completely and place with its seam side facing down on a serving platter. Refrigerate until use. It can last for 3 days.
4. Serve with sauce. Store the leftover sauce in an airtight container. It can last for a week.

Tip: You can serve it over any other whole grain wraps or use lettuce leaves to wrap.

Marinated Tempeh Wraps

Number of servings: 12

Nutritional values per serving: 1 wrap without vegan yogurt sauce

Calories – 200, Fat – 9.3 g, Carbohydrate – 35.8 g, Fiber – 3 g, Protein – 13 g

Ingredients:

For marinated tempeh:

- 2 packages tempeh (8 ounces each), drained, sliced
- ½ tablespoon apple cider vinegar
- 2 tablespoons tahini
- 2 teaspoons garlic powder
- 2 teaspoons ginger powder (optional)
- 2 teaspoons onion powder
- 4 tablespoons soy sauce
- 2 tablespoons agave nectar

For wraps:

- 1 red onion, thinly sliced
- 2 red bell peppers, thinly sliced

- 6 cups chopped lettuce
- 4 carrots, julienned
- 12 wraps or tortillas
- Oil free vegan yogurt sauce to taste (optional)

Directions:

1. Add soy sauce, garlic powder, ginger powder, onion powder, tamari, vinegar, agave, tahini, and salt into a bowl and whisk well.
2. Add tempeh and marinate for 1-8 hours.
3. Line a baking sheet with parchment paper. Remove the tempeh from the marinade and place on the baking sheet. Spread it evenly.
4. Bake in a preheated oven at 400° F until golden brown.
5. Place the wraps on your countertop. Scatter all the vegetables and tempeh over the wraps. Drizzle some vegan yogurt sauce if using.
6. Wrap and heat them in a pan if you prefer hot wraps. I prefer mine at room temperature.

Tip: You can swap tempeh for seitan. You can cook the tempeh in a pan if you do not want to bake it.

Vegan Mediterranean Wraps

Number of servings: 2

Nutritional values per serving: 1 wrap

Calories – 347, Fat – 8 g, Carbohydrate – 55 g, Fiber – 8 g, Protein – 12 g

Ingredients:

- 1 small cucumber, grate half and dice half
- 1 small tomato, diced
- 1/8 green bell pepper, diced
- 1/8 red onion, diced
- ½ jar (from a 19 ounces jar) chickpeas, drained

- 1 tablespoon chopped fresh dill
- ½ tablespoon lemon juice
- 1 cup chopped lettuce
- Salt to taste
- 2 tablespoons chopped kalamata olives
- 3.5 ounces soy yogurt or any other vegan yogurt
- 2 small cloves garlic, peeled, minced
- Pepper to taste
- 2 large tortillas

Directions:

1. Sprinkle a large pinch salt over the grated cucumber and place in a strainer. Place the strainer on top of a bowl. Let it drain for 15 minutes. Squeeze off the excess moisture.
2. To make tzatziki sauce: Add grated cucumber, dill, salt, pepper, lemon juice, garlic and yogurt into a bowl and stir.
3. Add chickpeas into a bowl and mash with a fork.
4. Mix together diced cucumber, tomato, olives and lettuce into a bowl and toss.
5. Spread the tortillas on your countertop. Divide the vegetable mixture and chickpeas among the tortillas.
6. Spoon some tzatziki sauce over the chickpeas. Wrap and place with its seam side facing down.
7. Heat the wrap in a pan if desired.
8. Serve with some more tzatziki sauce if desired.

Jackfruit wrap

Number of servings: 2

Nutritional values per serving: 1 wrap

Calories – 370, Fat – 14 g, Carbohydrate – 50 g, Fiber – NA g, Protein – 4 g

Ingredients:

- ½ can (from a 20 ounces can) green jackfruit, drained, rinsed
- ¼ teaspoon garlic powder
- ½ teaspoon onion powder
- ¼ cup BBQ sauce
- ¼ cup vegetable broth
- Salt to taste
- 1 cup shredded Romaine lettuce
- 1 small red onion, sliced
- 1 small tomato, sliced
- Few avocado slices
- 2 large gluten-free tortillas

For garlic aioli sauce:

- 2 tablespoons vegan mayonnaise
- 1 small clove garlic, crushed
- ¼ teaspoon lemon juice or to taste
- Salt to taste

Directions:

1. Add jackfruit into a bowl. Sprinkle onion powder, and garlic powder and toss well.
2. Place a skillet over medium heat. Add broth, jackfruit and BBQ sauce and mix well.
3. Cover and cook until jackfruit is tender. Remove the jackfruit and place on your cutting board. Shred the jackfruit with a pair of forks.
4. Meanwhile, make the garlic aioli by mixing together all the ingredients for aioli in a bowl.
5. Warm the tortillas and place on your countertop. Spread garlic aioli sauce on the tortillas. Divide the lettuce, tomato, avocado and onion slices among the tortillas.
6. Divide the jackfruit among the tortillas. Wrap like a burrito.
7. Cut into 2 halves and serve.

Tip: You can use any other sauce of your choice instead of garlic aioli. I keep trying a new sauce each time.

Supreme Crunch Wrap

Number of servings: 3

Nutritional values per serving: 1 wrap

Calories – 545, Fat – 26.7 g, Carbohydrate – 59.1 g, Fiber – NA, Protein – 17.9 g

Ingredients:

For spicy sofritas tofu:

- 1 ½ tablespoons olive oil
- 1 tablespoon taco seasoning
- ¼ cup salsa
- 8 ounces extra-firm tofu, pressed of excess moisture
- 1 chipotle pepper, minced
- 3 large flour tortillas

For cashew queso:

- ½ cup cashews
- ½ can diced green chilies
- ¼ cup water
- ½ teaspoon taco seasoning
- Salt to taste

For toppings: As required

- Tostadas or tortilla chips, broken into smaller pieces
- Roasted vegetables
- Avocado slices
- Black beans
- Tomatoes

- Salsa
- Cabbage slaw
- Cilantro
- Lettuce leaves etc.

Directions:

1. To make sofritas tofu: Place a skillet over medium heat. Add oil. When the oil is heated, add tofu and cook for a few minutes. Break it simultaneously as it cooks.
2. Stir in taco seasoning, salsa, chipotle pepper, and salt. Heat thoroughly. If you think that the mixture is getting stuck, add a little more oil.
3. Now cook for about 8-10 minutes. Do not stir for this time. The underside will be brown and crunchy. Flip sides and cook again until brown and crunchy.
4. Meanwhile, make cashew queso by adding all the ingredients into a blender. Blend until smooth.
5. Place the tortillas on your countertop. Divide the tofu among the tortillas.
6. Spoon cashew queso. Place tostadas and other toppings of your choice.
7. Wrap and place, with its seam side facing down.
8. Place a nonstick skillet over medium heat. Add a little oil. When the oil is heated, place the wrap and cook until golden brown all over. First, cook it with the seam side facing down.
9. Cut into 2 halves and serve.

Tip: I recommend that you use tostadas or tortilla chips as it makes the crunch wrap even crunchier.

Bacon and Edamame Wraps

Number of servings: 2

Nutritional values per serving:

Calories – 222, Fat – 7 g, Carbohydrate – 24 g, Fiber – 13 g, Protein – 16 g

Ingredients:

- 2.5 ounces fresh or frozen edamame
- 1 tablespoon chopped cilantro
- 1 tablespoon water
- 2 slices soy bacon
- 1 cup torn, mixed salad greens
- 1 small jalapeño, deseeded, chopped
- 1 tablespoon lemon juice
- 2 small cloves garlic, halved
- 2 whole wheat tortillas (8 inches each)
- 1 medium tomato, deseeded, chopped
- Salt to taste

Directions:

1. Follow the instructions on the package and cook the edamame. Rinse in cold water and drain.
2. Transfer into a blender. Add cilantro, chili pepper, water, lemon juice, and garlic and blend until smooth.
3. Follow the instructions on the package and cook the soy bacon until crisp. Remove onto a plate lined with paper towels. When cool enough to handle, chop into smaller pieces.
4. Spread the tortillas on your countertop. Spread 4 tablespoons of the edamame mixture on each.
5. Divide equally and place – salad, greens, tomatoes, and bacon, on the lower third portion of the tortillas, closest to you. Roll place with its seam side facing down.

Tempeh Sloppy Joes

Number of servings: 2

Nutritional values per serving:

Calories – 273, Fat – 7.9 g, Carbohydrate – 36.6 g, Fiber – 6.3 g, Protein – 17.6 g

Ingredients:

- 4 ounces tempeh, chopped
- ½ small onion, chopped
- ½ cup water, divided
- ½ green bell pepper, chopped
- ½ can (from an 8 ounces can) tomato sauce
- 1 tablespoon ketchup
- ½ tablespoon apple cider vinegar
- 1 tablespoon prepared mustard
- ½ tablespoon vegan Worcestershire sauce
- 2 cloves garlic, minced or ¼ teaspoon garlic powder
- 2 multigrain buns, split, to serve
- ½ tablespoon agave nectar
- ¼ teaspoon paprika
- 1 tablespoon chili powder
- 1/8 teaspoon ground cumin
- Salt to taste

Directions:

1. Place a skillet over medium heat. Add half the water. When the water is heated, add onion, and garlic and cook for a couple of minutes.
2. Add bell pepper and cook until tender.
3. Add remaining water and tempeh. Cook for a few minutes until the tempeh is cooked through.
4. Add rest of the ingredients and mix well. Increase heat to high and cook for 2-3 minutes, stirring frequently.
5. Split the buns and toast it if desired. Place the tempeh mixture on the bottom half of the buns. Cover with the top half of the buns.
6. Serve immediately.

Tip: You could swap tempeh with TVP or mock meat crumbles or lentils.

BBQ Lentil Sandwich

Number of servings:

Nutritional values per serving: Without bread or bun

Calories – 287, Fat – 0.7 g, Carbohydrate – 58.8 g, Fiber – 15.7 g, Protein – 13.1 g

Ingredients:

- 2 cups cooked green lentils

For BBQ sauce:

- 1 can (14 ounces) crushed tomatoes
- ¼ cup blackstrap molasses
- 1 small onion, quartered
- 2 cloves garlic, peeled
- ½ teaspoon dry mustard
- ¼ teaspoon red pepper flakes
- 1/8 teaspoon cayenne pepper
- 3 ounces canned tomato paste
- ½ tablespoon coconut sugar
- 1 tablespoon apple cider vinegar
- 1 tablespoon white vinegar
- ¼ teaspoon Himalayan pink salt or to taste
- ¼ teaspoon liquid smoke

Directions:

1. To make the sauce: Blend together all the ingredients for the sauce in a blender until smooth.
2. Transfer into a saucepan and place over medium heat.
3. When it begins to boil, lower the heat and cover with a lid. Simmer for about 20 minutes or until thick.
4. Remove from heat. Add lentils and mix well.
5. Serve over toasted bread or buns.

Tip: You can substitute green lentils with brown lentils.

Greek Avocado Sandwich

Number of servings: 2

Nutritional values per serving:

Calories – 560, Fat – 38.5 g, Carbohydrate – 48.3 g, Fiber – 15.1 g, Protein – 12.1 g

Ingredients:

- 4 slices soft whole wheat bread
- 2 tablespoons vegan basil pesto
- 1 small cucumber, thinly sliced
- 12 kalamata olives, pitted, thinly sliced
- Balsamic vinegar, to drizzle
- 1 avocado, peeled, pitted, mashed
- Jarred, roasted red bell pepper, as required
- 1 cup spring mix
- 1 red onion, thinly sliced into rounds

Directions:

1. Spread the mashed avocado on 2 slices of bread.
2. Place a layer of roasted red bell pepper.
3. Layer with cucumber slices followed onion, olives and finally spring mix.
4. Drizzle vinegar on top.
5. Spread the pesto on the remaining 2 slices of bread. Cover the sandwiches with these 2 slices of bread, with pesto side facing down.
6. Cut into desired shape and serve.

Grilled Nutella Banana Sandwich

Number of servings: 2

Nutritional values per serving: Without optional ingredients

Calories – 578, Fat – 29 g, Carbohydrate – 71 g, Fiber – 8.5 g, Protein – 10.6 g

Ingredients:

For sandwich:

- 4 slices rustic wheat bread
- 6 tablespoons vegan nutella
- 2 tablespoons coconut oil
- 2 bananas, sliced

Optional ingredients:

- 1 teaspoon coconut sugar
- ½ teaspoon ground cinnamon
- Salted peanut butter
- Strawberry slices

Directions:

1. Place a skillet over medium heat. If you have a cast-iron skillet, then there is nothing better than that.
2. Spread 1 ½ tablespoons nutella on each of the bread slices.
3. Place banana slices on 2 of the bread slices. Place optional ingredients if using. Cover with the remaining 2 bread slices, with the nutella side facing down.
4. Brush ½ tablespoon oil on the outer part of the sandwiches (½ tablespoon on each bread slice) and place on the heated pan.
5. Cook until the underside is golden brown and crisp. Flip sides and cook the other side until golden brown
6. Cut into the desired shape and serve.

Tip: The bananas should be ripe but firm as well.

Club Sandwich

Number of servings:

Nutritional values per serving:

Calories – 816.5, Fat – 39.9 g, Carbohydrate – 93.3 g, Fiber – 14.7 g, Protein – 29.7 g

Ingredients:

- 4 slices whole-wheat bread, toasted
- A few iceberg lettuce leaves
- 1 avocado, peeled, pitted, sliced
- 2 handfuls rocket salad
- A few fresh basil leaves
- 1 red onion, sliced
- 2 tablespoons vegan butter
- 2 tablespoons oil
- 4 tablespoons maple syrup
- 4 tablespoons soy sauce
- Garlic powder to taste
- 2 slices tofu
- 1 tomato, sliced
- Salt to taste

Directions:

1. Add soy sauce, maple syrup, garlic powder, and salt into a shallow bowl and stir.
2. Place tofu in it. Turn the tofu around once so that tofu is coated with the marinade. Let it marinate for 15 minutes.
3. Place a pan over medium heat. Add oil. When the oil is hot,
4. Add tofu. Fry until golden brown. Flip sides and cook the other side until golden brown. Remove from the pan and keep aside.
5. Toast the bread slices to the desired doneness.
6. Spread ½ tablespoon vegan butter on one side of all the slices of bread.
7. Lay lettuce leaves on 2 slices of bread. Place the tomato, avocado and tofu slices over it.

8. Place 3-4 basil leaves and close the sandwiches with remaining bread slices, with the buttered side facing down. Cut into the shape you desire and serve.

Four Layered Sandwich

Number of servings: 8

Nutritional values per serving:

Calories – 500, Fat – 26 g, Carbohydrate – 56 g, Fiber – 7 g, Protein – 18 g

Ingredients:

For sun-dried tomato hemp basil pesto:

- 2 large cloves garlic
- ½ cup oil-packed, sun-dried tomatoes
- ¼ cup lemon juice
- ¼ cup extra-virgin olive oil
- Freshly ground pepper to taste
- 2 cups fresh basil leaves
- ½ cup hulled hemp seeds
- ¼ cup water
- ½ teaspoon salt or taste

For the sandwich:

- 16 slices sprouted-grain bread, toasted
- 4 tablespoons sun-dried tomato hemp basil pesto
- 4 thin tomato slices
- A pinch of red pepper flakes
- 4 tablespoons hummus
- 1 avocado, thinly sliced
- Lettuce leaves
- Salt to taste
- Pepper to taste

Directions:

1. To make pesto: Blend together all the ingredients of the pesto in a blender until smooth.
2. Toast the bread to the desired doneness.
3. Spread the hummus over 8 slices of toasted bread. On the other 8 slices, apply pesto.
4. Place lettuce leaves, tomato, and avocado on the slices of bread with hummus. Sprinkle red pepper flakes, salt, and pepper. Cover with the remaining 8 slices of bread.
5. Cut into desired shapes and serve.

Chapter Twelve: Vegan Soup, Stews, and Chili Recipes

Spicy Black Bean Soup

Number of servings: 4

Nutritional values per serving:

Calories – 536, Fat – 22 g, Carbohydrate – 65 g, Fiber – 20 g, Protein – 21 g

Ingredients:

- 1 large onion, finely chopped
- 2 tablespoons olive oil
- 2 jalapeño peppers, deseeded, minced
- 2 red bell peppers, chopped
- 2 cups vegetable broth
- 3 teaspoons freshly ground cumin
- 2 tablespoons balsamic vinegar
- 1 Hungarian pepper, deseeded, minced
- 4 cloves garlic, minced
- 2 cans (15 ounces each) black beans
- 1 avocado, peeled, pitted, chopped
- Salt to taste
- Pepper to taste
- 2 tablespoons fresh cilantro, chopped
- 4 tortillas

Directions:

1. Mash about 1 can of black beans. Add garlic to it and stir. Set aside.
2. Place a heavy-bottomed pot over medium heat. Add oil. When the oil is heated, add onions, peppers (all the varieties) and cumin and sauté until the vegetables are soft.

3. Add rest of the ingredients except cilantro and bring to a boil.
4. Ladle into soup bowls and serve hot garnished with cilantro.

Tip: You can substitute these beans with any other beans of your choice. You can add some vegetables if desired. I generally add some carrots.

Red Curry Quinoa Soup

Number of servings: 3

Nutritional values per serving:

Calories – 164, Fat – 4 g, Carbohydrate – 26 g, Fiber – NA, Protein – 6 g

Ingredients:

- ½ tablespoon olive oil
- 1 small green bell pepper, deseeded, chopped
- 1 medium yellow onion, chopped
- 1 small sweet potato, chopped (about ¾ cup)
- ½ tablespoon red curry paste
- ½ cup quinoa
- 1 tablespoon lime juice
- A handful fresh cilantro, chopped
- 1 clove garlic, chopped
- 1 teaspoon fresh ginger, peeled, chopped
- 2 cups vegetable broth or water
- Salt to taste

Directions:

1. Place a pot over medium-high heat. Add oil. When the oil is heated, add onion, sweet potato and bell pepper.
2. Sauté for about 10 minutes.
3. Stir in ginger, garlic and curry paste. Sauté until aromatic.
4. Add quinoa and stir-fry for a minute.

5. Add broth and stir.
6. When it begins to boil, lower the heat and cook until sweet potatoes and quinoa are cooked.
7. Turn off the heat. Stir in lime juice and salt.
8. Ladle into soup bowls. Sprinkle cilantro on top and serve.

Split Pea Soup

Number of servings: 3

Nutritional values per serving:

Calories – 163, Fat – 3 g, Carbohydrate – 29 g, Fiber – 5 g, Protein – 7 g

Ingredients:

- ½ tablespoon canola oil
- 1 medium white onion, finely chopped
- 1 small stalk celery, sliced
- 2 cups vegetable broth
- ¾ cups green split peas, rinsed
- ½ small russet potato, cubed
- ½ teaspoon ground cumin
- Freshly ground pepper to taste
- 1 cup water
- Salt to taste
- 1 small carrot, chopped

Directions:

1. Place a soup pot over medium heat. Add oil. When the oil is heated, add onion, garlic, celery, and carrots and sauté for 3-4 minutes.
2. Add rest of the ingredients in a large pot and stir.
3. Cook until the split peas and potatoes are tender. Add more water if required.
4. Mix well. Ladle into soup bowls and serve hot.

Tip: You can pair this soup with some bread and salad of your choice to make a complete meal.

Tofu Noodle Soup

Number of servings: 8

Nutritional values per serving:

Calories – 404, Fat – 13 g, Carbohydrate – 55 g, Fiber – 5 g, Protein – 17 g

Ingredients:

- 1 large head broccoli, cut into florets
- 2 blocks (14 ounces each) firm tofu, drained, pressed of excess moisture
- 2 teaspoons coconut oil
- 3 tablespoons olive oil
- 2 cups diced celery
- 2 cups chopped carrots
- 2 large onions, thinly sliced
- ¼ teaspoon black pepper
- ¼ teaspoon white pepper
- 4 tablespoons soy sauce
- 3 tablespoons rice vinegar (optional)
- 1 teaspoon red chili flakes
- 2 tablespoons nutritional yeast
- Salt to taste
- 16 ounces brown rice elbow pasta

Directions:

1. Spread the tofu cubes on a lined baking sheet.
2. Bake in a preheated oven at 400° F until light brown.

3. Place a large pot over medium-high heat. Add coconut oil and olive oil. When it is heated, add celery, onion and carrot and sauté for about 4-5 minutes.
4. Add garlic, and all the spices. Sauté for a few seconds until aromatic.
5. Add tofu, pasta, and broccoli and stir-fry for a couple of minutes.
6. Add the rest of the ingredients and cook pasta until is al dente.
7. Ladle into soup bowls and serve.

Tip: You can use any other variety of pasta or noodles of your choice. You can add 1-2 colored bell peppers to make it more colorful.

Hot and Sour Soup

Number of servings: 8

Nutritional values per serving:

Calories – 208, Fat – 7.4 g, Carbohydrate – 21.6 g, Fiber – 5.4 g, Protein – 19.2 g

Ingredients:

- 8 cloves garlic, minced
- 4 tablespoons grated ginger, divided
- 2 packages (10 ounces each) mushrooms, sliced
- 16 fresh shiitake mushrooms, sliced
- 2 cans (8 ounces each) bamboo shoots, drained, julienned
- 2 package (15 ounces each) firm or silken tofu, chopped into small cubes
- 3 cups frozen peas
- 8 cups water
- 4 tablespoons vegan chicken-flavored bouillon
- 2 teaspoons chili paste
- 4 tablespoons soy sauce or tamari
- 4 tablespoons rice wine vinegar
- 2 teaspoons sesame oil + extra to drizzle

Directions:

1. Add all the ingredients except half the ginger and peas into a soup pot.

2. Place the pot over medium heat. When it begins to boil, lower the heat and cook until slightly tender. Stir occasionally.
3. Add peas and half the ginger and stir. Cook for a minute.
4. Cover and let it sit for 5 minutes. Taste and adjust the seasoning if required.
5. Ladle into soup bowls and serve.

Tip: You can add onion, carrots, beans, and any other vegetables of your choice to make it healthier.

Spicy Sun-Dried Tomato Soup with White Beans & Swiss Chard

Number of servings: 4

Nutritional values per serving:

Calories – 169, Fat – 8 g, Carbohydrate – 21 g, Fiber – 6 g, Protein – 5 g

Ingredients:

- 1 tablespoon olive oil
- ¼ teaspoon red pepper flakes
- 1 medium carrot, sliced
- ½ small zucchini, sliced
- ¾ cup chopped onion
- 1 stalk celery, chopped
- 1 teaspoon minced fresh rosemary
- 1 can (15 ounces) diced tomatoes
- ¼ cup oil-packed sun-dried tomatoes, drained, chopped
- 1 tablespoon oil from oil packed sun-drained tomatoes
- ¼ teaspoon chopped thyme
- 2 cloves garlic, minced
- 1 cup vegetable broth
- ½ can (from a 15 ounces can) white beans or cannellini beans, rinsed, drained

- 3 ounces Swiss chard, chopped
- ½ cup torn basil

Directions:

1. Place a soup pot over medium heat. Add oil. When the oil is heated, add garlic and red pepper flakes and sauté until aromatic.
2. Add onion, carrots, zucchini, celery, and rosemary and sauté until onions turn translucent.
3. Stir in the broth, beans, and ½ can tomatoes. Mix well. Add some of the mixture into the blender. Add rest of the canned tomatoes, sundried tomatoes, and its oil and blend until smooth.
4. Pour it back into the pot.
5. Heat thoroughly. Add salt and pepper to taste. Let it simmer for a few minutes. Garnish with basil and serve.
6. Ladle into soup bowls.

Lentil Spinach Soup

Number of servings: 8

Nutritional values per serving:

Calories – 354, Fat – 12 g, Carbohydrate – 41 g, Fiber – 18 g, Protein – 21 g

Ingredients:

- 4 cups vegetable broth
- 1 teaspoon ground cumin
- Salt to taste
- Pepper to taste
- ½ cup water
- 6 tablespoons olive oil
- 2 whole carrots, peeled, chopped
- 2 tablespoons tomato paste
- ½ teaspoon smoked paprika

- ½ cup + 2 tablespoons dry lentils, green or brown or red, rinse
- 4 cups chopped spinach
- Juice of a lemon
- 1 medium onion, chopped
- 2-3 cloves garlic, minced
- 1 bay leaf

Directions:

1. Place a saucepan or soup pot over medium heat. Add oil. When the oil is heated, add onion and carrot and sauté until the onions are translucent.
2. Add garlic, paprika, cumin, and salt and sauté for a few seconds until fragrant.
3. Stir in the tomato paste and pepper and cook for a couple of minutes.
4. Add water, lentils, and broth and bring to the boil.
5. Lower the heat and cover with a lid. Simmer until the lentils are tender. Add more water or broth if required.
6. Add spinach and cook until spinach wilts. Turn off the heat. Add lemon juice and stir. Taste and add more seasonings or lemon juice if required.
7. Ladle into soup bowls and serve.

Tip: You could add a boiled and mashed potato for added thickness.

Potato, Bean and Kale Soup

Number of servings: 3

Nutritional values per serving:

Calories – 207, Fat – 1.3 g, Carbohydrate – 39.9 g, Fiber – 8.5 g, Protein – 11.1 g

Ingredients:

- 1 cup chopped onion
- 4 cups vegetable broth
- 1 can (15 ounces) pinto beans, drained or 1 ½ cups cooked pinto beans

- 3 cloves garlic, minced
- ½ pound small potatoes, chopped into bite-sized pieces
- 5 -6 cups chopped kale leaves, discard hard stems and ribs
- ½ teaspoon dried basil
- ½ teaspoon dried oregano
- ¼ teaspoon dried rosemary, crushed
- ¼ teaspoons red pepper flakes
- ¼ teaspoon fennel seeds
- ¼ cup nondairy milk of your choice (optional)
- 1 tablespoon nutritional yeast
- Salt to taste
- Pepper to taste

Directions:

1. Add all the ingredients except kale, milk, and nutritional yeast into a soup pot.
2. Place the pot over medium heat. Cover and cook until potatoes are tender.
3. Add kale and stir. Cover and cook for 5-8 minutes until kale is bright green in color and tender as well.
4. Add milk and nutritional yeast. Mix well.
5. Taste and adjust the seasoning if necessary.
6. Ladle into soup bowls and serve.

Tip: You can replace the broth with 4 cups water 1-2 bouillon cubes

Healthy Lentil Soup

Number of servings: 6

Nutritional values per serving:

Calories – 230, Fat – 3 g, Carbohydrate – 33 g, Fiber –15.6 g, Protein – 18.7g

Ingredients:

- 1 ½ teaspoons vegetable oil
- 2 medium carrots, sliced
- 1 ½ onions, chopped
- 1 ½ cups dry brown lentils, rinsed, soaked for about 2 hours
- 3 bay leaves
- 2 tablespoons lemon juice or to taste
- 6 cups vegetable broth
- ½ teaspoon dried thyme
- Salt to taste
- Pepper to taste

Directions:

1. Place a soup pot over medium heat. Add oil. When the oil is heated, add onions and sauté until translucent.
2. Add rest of the ingredients except lemon juice and stir.
3. When it begins to boil, lower the heat and cover with a lid. Simmer until the lentils are tender.
4. Add lemon juice and stir.
5. Ladle into soup bowls and serve.

Hearty Seitan Stew

Number of servings:

Nutritional values per serving:

Calories – 384, Fat – 1 g, Carbohydrate – 80 g, Fiber – 9 g, Protein – 16 g

Ingredients:

- 2 pounds seitan, chopped
- 10 cups vegetable broth
- 6 cloves garlic, minced
- 6 potatoes, chopped

- 3 large carrots, chopped
- 4 stalks celery, chopped
- Freshly ground pepper to taste
- Salt to taste
- 4 tomatoes, chopped
- ½ cup cornstarch mixed with ½ cup water
- 4 tablespoons soy sauce
- 6 cloves garlic, peeled, minced
- Olive oil, as required

Directions

1. Place a soup pot over medium heat. Add a little oil. When the oil is heated, add the seitan and sauté for a few minutes. This is optional.
2. Add rest of the ingredients except cornstarch mixture and stir. Cover and cook until the vegetables are tender.
3. Add cornstarch mixture and constantly stir until thick.
4. Ladle into soup bowls and serve.

Tip: Try replacing potatoes with sweet potatoes. You can also replace seitan with vegan sausages. You can find vegan sausage recipes in my other book – Vegan breakfast for Athletes and Plant-based breakfast recipes. You can find a few recipes there.

Gumbo

Number of servings: 4

Nutritional values per serving: Without rice

Calories – 193, Fat – 7 g, Carbohydrate – 14 g, Fiber – 16 g, Protein – 14 g

Ingredients:

For soy curls:

- 1 cup soy curls, soaked in warm water for 15 minutes

- ½ teaspoon garlic powder
- ½ teaspoon onion powder
- 2 teaspoons coconut aminos

For roux:

- 1 tablespoon all-purpose flour
- 1 tablespoon olive oil

For the base:

- ½ tablespoon nutritional yeast
- 2 cloves garlic, minced
- 1 small green bell pepper, chopped
- 1 stalk celery, chopped
- 1 small onion, chopped
- 1 green onion, chopped
- 1 teaspoon Creole seasoning
- ½ teaspoon dried parsley flakes
- Cayenne pepper to taste
- ½ teaspoon dried thyme
- 1 cup thickly sliced okra
- 2 vegan sausages, cut into slices diagonally
- 2 cups vegetable broth
- 1 bay leaf
- Salt to taste
- Pepper to taste
- A dash of hot sauce to serve (optional)
- ½ can (from a 14.5 ounces can) diced tomatoes

Directions:

1. For soy curls: Drain the soy curls and place in a bowl. Add rest of the ingredients and toss well. Set aside.
2. For roux: Place a saucepan over medium heat. Add oil. When the oil is heated, add flour and continuously stir until it turns brown in color.

3. Add nutritional yeast, onion, bell pepper, celery, bell pepper, green onion, and garlic and sauté until onions are translucent.
4. Add tomatoes, spices, herbs, and broth constantly stirring and bring to a boil.
5. Lower the heat and let it simmer for 5-6 minutes.
6. Meanwhile, place a pan over medium heat. Add a little oil and cook the sausages until brown. Transfer into the saucepan. Also, add the soy curls and okra. Simmer until okra is tender.
7. Discard the bay leaf. Taste and adjust the seasonings if necessary.
8. Serve over hot cooked rice. Drizzle a bit of hot sauce on top.

Tip: You can add Cajun seasoning instead of Creole seasoning and also add other vegetables like mushrooms, zucchini carrots, etc. You can use canned or cooked beans for extra protein.

Vegetable Stew

Number of servings: 3

Nutritional values per serving:

Calories – 274, Fat – 8 g, Carbohydrate – 40 g, Fiber – NA, Protein – 11 g

Ingredients:

- 1 tablespoon olive oil
- 1 small red bell pepper, chopped
- 1 small green bell pepper, chopped
- 1 small onion, chopped
- 1 clove garlic, peeled, chopped
- ½ can (from a 14.5 ounces can) diced tomatoes
- ½ tablespoon curry powder
- ½ tablespoon finely chopped fresh ginger
- Pepper to taste
- 5 ounces baby spinach

- 1 small head cauliflower, cut into florets
- A pinch ground cayenne pepper
- ½ cup light coconut milk
- 1 can (15 ounces) chickpeas, drained, rinsed
- ½ tablespoon pure maple syrup
- Salt or Himalayan pink salt to taste

Directions:

1. Place a soup pot over medium-high heat. Add oil. When the oil is heated, add onions and bell peppers and cook until onions are soft.
2. Add garlic and sauté until fragrant.
3. Add spices, cauliflower, broth, tomatoes with its juice and chickpeas into it. Mix well.
4. Cover and cook until cauliflower is tender.
5. Stir in the spinach and coconut milk.
6. Cover and cook until spinach wilts.
7. Ladle into soup bowls and serve.

Vegan Chili

Number of servings: 5

Nutritional values per serving:

Nutritional values per serving:

Calories – 260.37, Fat – 10.96 g, Carbohydrate – 27.39 g, Fiber – NA, Protein – 14.07 g

Ingredients:

- 1 tablespoon olive oil
- ½ cup chopped red bell pepper
- ½ package (6.5 ounces) vegan sausage, chopped
- ¼ cup white wine
- ½ teaspoon salt or to taste
- ½ teaspoon crushed red pepper

- 1 cup chopped tomato
- Freshly ground pepper to taste
- ½ teaspoon dried ground sage
- 3 cups vegetable stock
- 1 can (15 ounces) unsalted kidney beans, rinsed, drained, divided
- 1 ½ cans (15 ounces each) cannellini beans, rinsed, drained, divided
- 1 cup chopped kale, discard hard stems and ribs
- ½ cup chopped onion
- ½ tablespoon chopped garlic

Directions:

1. Place a Dutch oven or soup pot over medium-high heat. Add oil. When the oil is heated, add onions, garlic, sausage, and bell pepper. Sauté for 3-4 minutes.
2. Add tomatoes, spices, salt, wine, and sage. Boil until the wine reduces to half its original quantity.
3. Add stock and stir. Add ½ can kidney beans and ¾ can cannellini beans into a bowl and mash with a potato masher. Add into the pot. Also add the remaining beans. Let it simmer for 5-8 minutes. Stir occasionally.
4. Add kale and cook until it wilts. Add oregano and stir.
5. Ladle into soup bowls and serve.

Tofu Chili

Number of servings: 4

Nutritional values per serving:

Calories – 521, Fat – 11 g, Carbohydrate – 82 g, Fiber – 24 g, Protein – 31 g

Ingredients:

- 1 ½ tablespoons olive oil
- 1 medium onion, chopped
- 2 cloves garlic, minced

- 1 ½ tablespoons chili powder
- ¼ teaspoon cayenne pepper
- Salt to taste
- Pepper to taste
- ½ tablespoon ground cumin
- ½ can (from a 28 ounces can) whole or diced tomatoes with its liquid
- ½ can (from a 15 ounces can) kidney beans, drained, rinsed
- ½ can (from a 14 ounces can) tomato sauce
- ½ tablespoon sugar (optional)
- ½ cup sliced mushrooms
- 7 ounces extra-firm tofu, crumbled
- ½ green bell pepper, chopped
- 1 cup vegetable broth
- 2 tablespoons fresh cilantro, chopped

Directions:

1. Place a heavy-bottomed pot over medium heat. Add oil. When the oil is heated, add tofu and cook until light brown.
2. Add onion, mushroom, bell pepper, all the spices and garlic sauté until vegetables are slightly tender.
3. Add rest of the ingredients except cilantro and stir.
4. When it begins to boil, lower the heat and cover with a lid.
5. Simmer for about a 30-40 minutes. Stir occasionally.
6. Ladle into bowls. Garnish with cilantro and serve.

Easy Vegan Chili Sin Carne

Number of servings: 2

Nutritional values per serving: Without optional ingredients and rice

Calories – 340, Fat NA, Carbohydrate – 42 g, Fiber – 18 g, Protein – 25 g

Ingredients:

For chili:

- 1 tablespoon olive oil
- 1 medium red onion, thinly sliced
- 2 cloves garlic, minced
- 1 ½ tablespoons chili powder
- ¼ teaspoon cayenne pepper
- Salt to taste
- ½ tablespoon ground cumin
- 1 stalk celery, finely chopped
- 1 small red bell pepper, chopped
- ½ can (from a 15 ounces can) kidney beans, drained, rinsed
- ½ package (from a 14.5 ounces package) frozen soy mince
- ½ cup vegetable broth
- ½ can (from a 28 ounces can) diced tomatoes with its liquid
- 1.8 ounces split red lentils

Optional ingredients:

- ½ teaspoon miso paste
- A handful fresh cilantro, chopped
- 1 tablespoon balsamic vinegar

To serve:

- Cooked basmati rice
- Lime juice to drizzle
- Handful cilantro, chopped

Directions:

1. Place a soup pot over medium heat. Add oil. When the oil is heated, add the vegetables and sauté until slightly tender
2. Add salt and spices and mix well.
3. Add rest of the ingredients for chili and stir. When it begins to boil, lower the heat.

4. Cover and cook until thick. Turn off the heat.
5. Add optional ingredients and stir.
6. Serve with rice, if desired

Buffalo Cauliflower Chili

Number of servings: 8

Nutritional values per serving: Without bread

Calories – 333.6, Fat – 2.9 g, Carbohydrate – 62.9 g, Fiber – 19.8 g, Protein – 18.3 g

Ingredients:

- 8 cups cauliflower florets, cut into bite-size pieces
- 4 cans (15 ounces each) cannellini beans, drained, rinsed
- 2 cans (4 ounces each) diced green chilies
- 4 tablespoons brown sugar
- 4 teaspoons ground cumin
- Salt to taste
- 2 large onions, chopped
- 2 cans (28 ounces each) diced tomatoes with its juice
- 1 cup Frank's red hot sauce
- 2 tablespoons chili powder
- 4 teaspoons ground cumin
- Salt to taste

Directions:

1. Place a soup pot over medium heat. Spray some cooking spray.
2. Add onion and sauté until translucent.
3. Add rest of the ingredients and stir.
4. Cover and cook until cauliflower is tender.
5. Ladle into bowls and serve with some crusty bread.

Chapter Thirteen: Rice Recipes

Curried Pumpkin and Mushroom Risotto

Number of servings: 4

Nutritional values per serving:

Nutritional values per serving: ½ cup

Calories – 153, Fat – 6 g, Carbohydrate – 22 g, Fiber – 3 g, Protein – 6 g

Ingredients:

- 1 medium leek, trimmed, halved, thinly slice the white parts only
- 8 ounces fresh mushrooms, sliced
- 1 1/3 cups low sodium vegetable broth, warmed + more if required
- 6 tablespoons canned pumpkin
- ½ tablespoon canola oil
- 1 teaspoon curry powder
- 6 tablespoons Arborio rice
- A handful fresh parsley, chopped (optional)
- 2 tablespoons pumpkin seeds (pepitas), toasted

Directions:

1. Place a skillet over medium-high heat. Add oil. When the oil is heated, add leeks and cook for 2-3 minutes. Add mushrooms and cook until slightly soft.
2. Add curry powder and stir for a few seconds until fragrant.
3. Add rice and stir fry for a couple of minutes.
4. Pour ½ cup of the broth and stir. In a while, the broth will be absorbed.
5. Repeat the above step until the rice is cooked. Use more broth if required.
6. Add pumpkin and stir. Heat thoroughly.
7. Garnish with pumpkin seeds and parsley and serve.

Roasted Vegetable and Spinach Risotto

Number of servings: 8

Nutritional values per serving:

Calories – 501, Fat – 15 g, Carbohydrate – 80 g, Fiber – 5.1 g, Protein – 12.4 g

Ingredients:

For roast vegetables:

- 1 pound Kabocha squash or Buttercup squash or Japanese pumpkin, cut into ½ inch pieces
- 2 tablespoons olive oil
- 1 pound carrots, cut into ½ inch pieces
- Salt to taste
- Pepper to taste

For risotto:

- 3 cups medium-grain white rice
- 2 tablespoons garlic infused oil
- 8 cups vegetable stock
- 5 tablespoons lemon juice
- 1/3 cup fresh cilantro, chopped
- 1 cup leeks, green parts only, chopped
- 2 tablespoons dairy-free spread or olive oil or vegan butter
- 4 teaspoons lemon zest, grated
- 8 cups shredded spinach
- 3.5 ounces soy-based vegan cheese, grated (optional)

Directions:

1. Place squash and carrots in a baking dish. Drizzle oil over it. Sprinkle salt and pepper and toss well.
2. Roast in a preheated oven at 400° F for 20-25 minutes or until brown and cooked.

3. Stir a couple of times while roasting.
4. To make risotto: Place a large saucepan over medium heat. Add dairy-free spread and garlic-infused oil. When the oil is heated, add rice and cook until it is well coated with the oil.
5. Add stock, a little at a time and cook until dry each time. Keep doing this until the rice is cooked.
6. Add spinach, lemon zest, lemon juice, salt, and pepper and mix well.
7. Add the roasted vegetables, cilantro, and cheese if using and mix until well combined.
8. Spoon into bowls and serve.

Quick Mexican Brown Rice

Number of servings:

Nutritional values per serving:

Calories – 200, Fat – 3.5 g, Carbohydrate – 39 g, Fiber – 3 g, Protein – 5 g

Ingredients:

- 2 cups frozen or cooked brown rice
- 1 small onion, finely chopped
- ½ jalapeño, deseeded, minced
- 1 tablespoon tomato paste
- ¼ teaspoon cayenne pepper
- ¼ teaspoon ground cumin
- Freshly ground black pepper
- ¼ teaspoon smoked paprika
- 1 medium plum tomato, diced into small pieces
- 1 clove garlic, peeled, minced
- 1 teaspoon olive oil
- Salt to taste
- A handful fresh cilantro, chopped, to garnish

- Lime wedges to serve

Directions:

1. Thaw the rice if frozen.
2. Place a skillet or wok over medium-high heat. Add onions, tomatoes and jalapeño, and sauté until slightly soft.
3. Add garlic and sauté until fragrant.
4. Add rest of the ingredients except rice and stir. Add rice and mix well. Heat thoroughly
5. Sprinkle cilantro on top and serve with lime wedges.

Spanish rice

Number of servings: 8

Nutritional values per serving:

Calories – 270, Fat – 7.6 g, Carbohydrate – 45.7 g, Fiber – 2.5 g, Protein – 4.8 g

Ingredients:

- 1 green bell pepper, chopped
- 2 large onions, chopped
- 2 cups rice, rinsed, drained
- 4 tablespoons vegetable oil
- 2 cans (10 ounces each) tomatoes with green chilies
- 4 cups water
- 1 ½ teaspoons chili powder or to taste
- 2 teaspoons salt or to taste

Directions:

1. Place a large, deep skillet over medium heat. Add oil. When the oil is heated, add onions, bell pepper, and rice and stir-fry for 2-3 minutes.
2. Add rest of the ingredients and mix well.
3. When it begins to boil, lower the heat and cover with a lid.

4. Cook until dry.
5. Stir occasionally. Turn off the heat. Let it sit for about 10 minutes.
6. Fluff with a fork and serve.

Tip: You could add some tofu for added protein.

Coconut Rice with Snow Peas

Number of servings: 3

Nutritional values per serving:

Calories – 130, Fat – 3 g, Carbohydrate – 22 g, Fiber – 1 g, Protein – 3 g

Ingredients:

- ½ cup water
- 6 tablespoons uncooked, long-grain rice, rinsed
- 1 heaping cup sliced, fresh snow pea pods (2 inch pieces)
- ½ cup light coconut milk, unsweetened
- ¼ teaspoon salt or to taste
- 2 almonds, slivered, toasted

Directions:

1. Add all the ingredients except snow peas into a saucepan. Place the saucepan over medium heat.
2. When it begins to boil, lower the heat and cover with a lid. Simmer until nearly dry.
3. Scatter the pea pods on top. Cover and cook until rice is fully cooked and vegetables are crisp as well as tender.
4. Turn off the heat. Let it rest for 10 minutes.
5. Fluff with a fork and serve.

Asian-Style Fried Rice and Beans

Number of servings: 8

Nutritional values per serving:

Calories – 350, Fat – NA, Carbohydrate – 65 g, Fiber – 10 g, Protein – 11 g

Ingredients:

- 1 pineapple, peeled, cored or use 2 cans (8 ounces each) pineapple slices, chopped into 1 inch pieces
- 4 medium carrots, thinly sliced on the bias
- 4 teaspoons grated ginger
- 2 tablespoons vegetable oil
- 4 cups cooked brown rice
- 2 cups frozen peas, thawed
- 2/3 cup chopped fresh cilantro + extra to garnish
- 2 cans (15 ounces each) chickpeas, rinsed, drained
- 6 tablespoons soy sauce
- Juice of 2 limes
- Salt to taste (optional)

Directions:

1. Place a large nonstick pan or wok over medium heat. Add half the oil. When the oil is heated, add pineapple and cook until golden brown all over. Remove the pineapple with a slotted spoon and place on a plate.
2. Add remaining oil. When the oil is heated, add carrots and sauté until crisp as well as tender.
3. Stir in the ginger and garlic and cook for a few seconds until aromatic.
4. Add rice, peas, soy sauce, and chickpeas. Stir-fry for a few minutes until well heated.
5. Add cilantro and pineapple and toss well. Let it blend with the rice for a couple of minutes.
6. Garnish with cilantro and serve hot.

Mexican Rice with Black Beans and Corn

Number of servings: 8

Nutritional values per serving:

Calories – 448, Fat – 1 g, Carbohydrate – 95 g, Fiber – 11 g, Protein – 14 g

Ingredients:

- 2 onions, chopped
- 2 teaspoons ground cumin
- 1 teaspoon chili flakes
- 3 cups basmati rice or any other long-grain rice
- 4 ½ cups water
- 1 cup corn
- ¼ cup fresh cilantro, chopped
- 6 cloves garlic, grated
- 5-6 teaspoons smoked paprika or to taste
- 1 red bell pepper, diced
- 1 yellow bell pepper, diced
- 23.7 ounces passata or 2 cans (14.5 ounces each) chopped tomatoes
- Salt to taste
- Pepper to taste
- 2 cans (14.5 ounces each) black beans, rinsed, drained

To serve:

- A handful fresh cilantro, chopped
- Fresh chilies, sliced
- 1 spring onion, sliced

Directions:

1. Place a deep, wide pan or saucepan over medium heat. Add oil. When the oil is heated, add onion and sauté until translucent.

2. Add garlic, bell peppers and spices and stir for a couple of minutes.
3. Stir in the rice, water, passata, pepper, and salt. When it begins to boil, lower the heat and cover with a lid.
4. After about 10 minutes, add corn and black beans and stir. Cover and cook until rice is cooked. If you think that the rice is uncooked, add some more water and cook.
5. Turn off the heat. Let it sit for 10 minutes.
6. Fluff with a fork. Sprinkle cilantro, chilies and spring onions on top and serve.

Tip: It goes well with roasted corn on the cob or sweet potatoes. You can also serve some chunky guacamole. It pairs perfectly with the rice.

Chapter Fourteen: Vegan Mock "Meat" Recipes

"Liverwurst"

Number of servings: 32

Nutritional values per serving:

Calories – 61.6, Fat – 2.9 g, Carbohydrate – 5.6 g, Fiber – 1.4 g, Protein – 4.4 g

Ingredients:

- 2 blocks extra-firm silken tofu
- Dark sesame oil, to grease
- 2 medium russet potatoes, scrubbed, cut into 1 inch cubes
- 1 medium onion, cut into 1 inch squares
- ½ cup whole wheat flour ½ cup soy sauce
- ¼ cup warm water
- 1 teaspoon organic sugar
- 1 cup raw shelled sunflower seeds
- ½ cup nutritional yeast
- 3 tablespoons lemon juice
- 4 cloves garlic, peeled
- 1 teaspoon dried thyme
- 1 teaspoon dried marjoram
- 1 teaspoon dried rosemary
- ¼ teaspoon ground allspice
- Freshly ground pepper to taste
- ¼ teaspoon freshly ground nutmeg
- Salt to taste

Directions:

1. Grease 4 nonstick loaf pans with dark sesame oil. Place parchment paper on the bottom of the loaf pans. Grease the parchment paper as well.
2. Add all the ingredients into a blender and blend until smooth.
3. Divide equally into the prepared loaf pans.
4. Cover the loaf pans with aluminum foil. Bake in batches if required.
5. Take a large baking pan and place the loaf pans in it. Pour enough hot water to cover 1 inch from the bottom of the loaf pan.
6. Bake in a preheated oven at 350° F for 50-60 minutes.
7. Remove from the oven and place on the wire rack to cool completely.
8. Run a knife around the edges of the loaf pan and loosen the liverwurst. Invert on to a plate. Cover with cling wrap, and place in the refrigerator until use. It can last for a week. Cut each loaf into 8 slices.
9. To freeze, cover liverwurst with foil and place in a Ziploc bag. Seal the bag and place in the freezer. It can last for 3 months.

Tip: You can replace flour with stone-ground cornmeal or soy flour or chickpea flour

Bolognese

Number of servings: 12

Nutritional values per serving:

Calories – 382.7, Fat – 4.2 g, Carbohydrate – 77.7 g, Fiber – 5.7 g, Protein – 17.3 g

Ingredients:

- 3-4 tablespoons olive oil
- 2 carrots, chopped
- 2 onions, chopped
- 4 cloves garlic, peeled, minced
- 2 tablespoons dried oregano
- 2 tablespoons dried basil
- 2 tablespoons dried thyme

- 2 teaspoons crushed red pepper flakes
- 2 bay leaves
- 2 cups dry textured vegetable protein, do not re-hydrate
- 2 cups vegetable stock
- 4 tablespoons nutritional yeast
- 1 cup chopped fresh basil or parsley
- 5-6 tablespoons soy sauce or tamari or coconut aminos
- 2 cans (6 ounces each) tomato paste
- 2 cans (28 ounces each) crushed tomatoes with its liquid
- Salt to taste
- Pepper to taste
- 2 pounds whole wheat spaghetti

Directions:

1. Place a Dutch oven over medium heat. Add oil. When the oil is heated, add onions and carrots and sauté until slightly soft.
2. Stir in some salt, pepper, crushed red pepper, and all the dried herbs. Mix well. If you find the mixture too dry, then add a little more oil.
3. Add garlic and sauté until fragrant. Stir in the textured vegetable protein and mix until well coated.
4. Stir in the soy sauce and vegetable broth. Mix well. Let it cook for a couple of minutes.
5. Add tomato paste and sauté for a couple of minutes. Add crushed tomatoes and mix well.
6. Lower the heat and simmer for a while.
7. Meanwhile, follow the instructions on the package and cook the spaghetti.
8. Serve over hot cooked spaghetti. Garnish with basil or parsley and serve.
9. Leftovers can be transferred into an airtight container and refrigerate until use. It can store for 4-5 days. Keep the Bolognese sauce and spaghetti in separate containers.

Tip: This pasta is great for parties. You can make it ahead of time. This dish is a favorite with my meat-eating friends, and they insist I make it at parties.

Mushroom Walnut Bolognese

Number of servings: 4

Nutritional values per serving:

Calories – 193, Fat – 10 g, Carbohydrate – 19 g, Fiber – 4 g, Protein – 6 g

Ingredients:

- 5 ounces crimini mushrooms, halved, cut into fine strips
- ½ cup finely chopped walnuts
- 2 small onions, cut into 2 inch pieces
- 1 rib celery, cut into 2 inch pieces
- 1 large clove garlic, peeled, finely chopped
- 1 ½ tablespoons tomato paste
- ½ teaspoon paprika
- Pepper to taste
- Salt to taste
- Red chili flakes to taste
- ½ cup dry red wine
- 1 can (14 ounces) whole tomatoes, crushed or chopped
- 2 tablespoons dried basil
- 2 tablespoons dried oregano
- ½ cup water
- Vegan Parmesan cheese to garnish

Directions:

1. Add mushrooms into the food processor bowl and process until finely ground. Do not grind for long. Transfer into a bowl.
2. Add walnuts into the food processor bowl and process until finely powdered.
3. Place a skillet over medium heat. Add a tablespoon of water.
4. Add mushrooms and walnuts and sauté for 7-8 minutes. When the mushrooms are dried and brown. Remove onto a plate.
5. Add onion, celery, carrot, and garlic into the food processor and process until roughly chopped.

6. Add into the skillet. Add a tablespoon of water and a large pinch salt. Cook until brown.
7. Push the vegetables to one side of the pan.
8. Add all the spices, herbs, and tomato paste in the center of the pan and mix well. Cook for a few minutes.
9. Add the tomatoes and red wine stir.
10. Lower the heat and cook for about 20 minutes. Add walnut mixture and cook for 5 more minutes.
11. Serve over pasta. Garnish with vegan Parmesan cheese.

Tip: You can try serving over polenta.

Cashew "Chicken" Stir Fry

Number of servings: 6

Nutritional values per serving: Without serving options

Calories – 295, Fat – 16 g, Carbohydrate – 28 g, Fiber – 4 g, Protein – 13 g

Ingredients:

- 4 tablespoons peanut oil
- 2 teaspoon minced fresh ginger
- 1 ½ cups sliced mushrooms
- 4 stalks celery, sliced
- 2/3 cup vegetable broth or water
- 2 tablespoons cornstarch mixed with 1/3 cup water
- 6 green onions, sliced (optional)
- 6 cloves garlic, minced
- 16 ounces firm or extra-firm tofu, pressed of excess moisture
- 2 cans (4 ounces each) bamboo shoots, drained, thinly sliced
- 1 red bell pepper, deseeded, chopped
- 1 green bell pepper, deseeded, chopped
- 4 tablespoons soy sauce

- 1 cup cashews

Directions:

1. Place a large skillet over medium heat. Add oil. When the oil is heated, add ginger and garlic and sauté for a couple of minutes until aromatic.
2. Add tofu and cook until slightly brown.
3. Stir in the bell peppers and celery and stir-fry for a couple of minutes.
4. Stir in the mushrooms and bamboo shoots.
5. Next, add in the broth and soy sauce and bring to a boil.
6. Pour the cornstarch mixture and constantly stir until thick. Add cashew and green onions and mix well.
7. Serve over rice or noodles or any other grain of your choice.

Tip: You can try replacing tofu with tempeh or seitan. I have tried it. Believe me, it tastes great.

Vegan Classic Meatloaf

Number of servings: 16

Nutritional values per serving:

Calories – 254, Fat – 5.8 g, Carbohydrate – 46.2 g, Fiber – 7.2 g, Protein – 8.4 g

Ingredients:

For chickpea meatloaf:

- 4 cans (14 ounces each) chickpeas, drained, rinsed or equivalent quantity of cooked chickpeas
- 4 stalks celery, chopped
- 4 cloves garlic, minced
- 1 cup plain soy or almond milk
- 4 teaspoons soy sauce or tamari
- 4 tablespoons ground flaxseeds
- 2 teaspoons liquid smoke

- 2 onions, diced
- 4 carrots, diced
- 4 cups whole wheat panko breadcrumbs
- 6 tablespoons vegan Worcestershire sauce
- 4 tablespoons olive oil
- 4 tablespoons tomato paste
- 1 teaspoon pepper powder or to taste

For maple glaze:

- 6 tablespoons tomato paste
- 3 tablespoons apple cider vinegar
- 1 ½ teaspoons paprika
- 3 tablespoons maple syrup
- 1 ½ tablespoons soy sauce or tamari

Directions:

1. Grease 2 loaf pans of 12 ounces each, with a little oil. Set aside.
2. Add all the ingredients of the meatloaf into the food processor bowl and process until chickpeas are finely chopped and not smooth. The mixture should be well combined. Do not pulse for long. Else you will end up in a soggy mess. Pulse in batches if required.
3. Transfer into a large bowl. Mix well. You can use your hands as it can bind well.
4. Transfer the mixture into the prepared loaf pans. Press the mixture into the pans.
5. Bake in a preheated oven at 375 º F for about 30-40 minutes.
6. Meanwhile, mix together all the ingredients of glaze in a bowl and set aside.
7. When the meatloaves are baked, pour it on top of the meatloaf, spread it evenly.
8. Bake for 20-30 minutes. When done, cool for at least 15 -20 minutes.
9. Slice and serve.

Tip: If you let the meatloaf cool completely, it slices better. In fact, if you make it a day earlier and cut it just before eating, the next day, it is perfect. Warm it if desired and serve.

Lentil Meatloaf

Number of servings: 16

Nutritional values per serving:

Calories –316, Fat – 11 g, Carbohydrate – 42 g, Fiber – 7 g, Protein – 8 g

Ingredients:

- 2 large butternut squashes, peeled, cubed
- 6 onions, chopped
- 4 sprigs rosemary, leaves chopped, + extra to garnish
- 2 teaspoons ground mace
- 4 packages (7 ounces each) cooked chestnuts
- 14 ounces whole-meal vegan breadcrumbs
- 6 tablespoons sunflower oil + extra to grease
- 1 ounce fresh sage leaves, set aside 20-25 and finely chop the remaining leaves
- 6 cloves garlic, crushed
- 4 tablespoons ground chia seeds
- 4 cans (14.5 ounces each) brown lentils, rinsed, drained
- 6 tablespoons rapeseed oil
- Salt to taste
- Pepper to taste

Directions:

1. Place the squashes in a baking dish. Drizzle 2 tablespoons oil and toss well. Spread it evenly.
2. Bake in a preheated oven at 350 º F for about 30 minutes or until cooked and golden brown.

3. Take 2 loaf pans (9 inches each) and line it with parchment paper.
4. Grease with a little oil on the bottom, as well as the sides of the dish.
5. Place a pan over medium-low heat. Add remaining oil. When the oil is heated, add onion and sauté until translucent.
6. Add chopped sage, mace, leaves of 2 sprigs rosemary and garlic and sauté until aromatic. Turn off the heat.
7. Add chia seeds and ½ cup water into a bowl and mix well. Set aside for 15 minutes. This is the flax egg.
8. In the meantime, add half the chestnuts, half the lentils, and half the roasted squash into the food processor bowl and process until the mixture is well combined.
9. Transfer into a bowl. Add sautéed onion mixture, flax egg, breadcrumbs, pepper and 2 teaspoons salt or to taste into a bowl. Mix until well incorporated.
10. Chop the remaining chestnuts and add into the bowl. Also, add the remaining lentils and mix gently.
11. Divide equally the mixture among the loaf pans. Press it well.
12. Cover the loaf pans with aluminum foil. Place in the refrigerator for 12-24 hours.
13. Place on the rack in the center of the oven.
14. Bake covered, in a preheated oven at 350º F for about 45 -60 minutes.
15. Remove from the oven and cool completely. Remove from the oven and loosen the edges of the loaves with a blunt knife. Invert onto plates. Peel off the parchment paper.
16. Meanwhile, place a small pan over medium heat. Add oil. When the oil is heated, add the whole sage leaves that were retained and remaining rosemary sprigs and cook for a minute.
17. Pour all over the loaves.
18. Cut each into 8 equal slices and serve.
19. Leftover meatloaf slices can be wrapped individually in plastic wrap and placed in freezer-safe bags. Freeze until use. It can last for a month.

Chickpea "Meat Balls" with Vegetable Marinara Sauce

Number of servings: 6

Nutritional values per serving: Without spaghetti

Calories – 754, Fat – 35 g, Carbohydrate – 64 g, Fiber – NA, Protein – 41 g

Ingredients:

For marinara sauce:

- 6 tablespoons extra-virgin olive oil
- 4 stalks celery, very finely chopped
- 4 bay leaves
- 2 teaspoons minced fresh thyme
- 2 large carrots, very finely chopped
- 8 cloves garlic, peeled, minced
- Salt to taste
- 1 ½ cups + 3 tablespoons vegan white wine
- 17.6 ounces fresh mushrooms, chopped
- 2 cans (14.5 ounces each) chopped tomatoes
- 2 vegetable stock cubes
- ½ cup finely chopped fresh basil
- 2 teaspoons freshly ground pepper
- 1 ½ cups + 3 tablespoons water
- 4 tablespoons tomato puree

For chickpea meatballs:

- 2 blocks extra-firm tofu (14 ounces each), pressed of excess moisture, crumbled
- 4 tablespoons light soy sauce or tamari
- 4 tablespoons dried porcini mushrooms
- ½ cup chopped fresh parsley
- 2 cans (14.5 ounces each) chickpeas, drained, rinsed
- 1 teaspoon chili powder or to taste
- Salt to taste
- Oil, to fry, as required
- 2 teaspoons vegetable bouillon powder

- 4 tablespoons dark soy sauce or tamari
- 2 small red onions, chopped
- 1 cup pistachio nuts
- 2 tablespoons paprika
- Freshly ground pepper to taste
- 2 cloves garlic, crushed or 2 teaspoons garlic powder

To serve:

- Spaghetti to serve

Directions:

1. To make the marinara sauce: Place a large pan over medium heat. Add oil. When the oil is heated, add all the vegetables except mushrooms, salt, thyme, and bay leaves and sauté for about 5 minutes.
2. Add white wine and pepper and stir. Scrape the bottom of the pan to remove any browned bits. Cover and cook until vegetables are tender.
3. Stir in the mushrooms and cook until vegetables are soft. Add rest of the ingredients and mix well.
4. Lower the heat. Cover with a lid and simmer for about 10 minutes. Uncover and simmer for another 10 minutes or until thick. Stir occasionally. Turn off the heat.
5. To make chickpea meatballs: Add tofu into a bowl. Add vegetable bouillon powder, light and dark soy sauce and mix well.
6. Transfer onto a baking sheet. Spread it evenly.
7. Bake in a preheated oven at 400° F for 35-45 minutes or until firm. Lower the temperature of the oven to 370° F.
8. Add dried mushrooms in the food processor bowl. Process until powdered.
9. Add onion, pistachio, paprika, pepper, garlic, parsley, chickpeas, chili powder, and salt and blend until thick and well combined.
10. Transfer into a large mixing bowl. Add tofu and mix well.
11. Make small balls of the mixture (about 1 ½ inches diameter) and place on a baking sheet.

12. Place a pan over medium heat. Add a few tablespoons oil. When the oil is heated, add meatballs and fry until brown all over. Transfer onto the baking sheet.
13. Bake in a preheated oven at 400° F for 20-30 minutes or until cooked through.
14. Add meatballs into the sauce and simmer for a couple of minutes.
15. Serve meatballs with sauce over spaghetti.
16. Garnish with parsley and serve.

Easy BBQ Flavored Baked Tofu

Number of servings: 8

Nutritional values per serving:

Calories – 231, Fat – 7 g, Carbohydrate – 32 g, Fiber – 1 g, Protein – 12 g

Ingredients:

- 2 cups BBQ sauce
- 2 blocks (1 pound each) firm or extra-firm tofu, pressed of excess moisture, cut into ½ inch thick slices

Directions:

1. Place a sheet of foil on a baking sheet. Spread some sauce on the baking sheet.
2. Place the tofu on the baking sheet.
3. Spread some sauce on the top of the tofu.
4. Bake in a preheated oven at 350° F for about 60 minutes.

Tip: You can serve with salad or place it as a filling in sandwiches with other ingredients like tomatoes, onions, and lettuce. You can spread some mayonnaise or vegan butter on the bread and place the tofu and other fillings etc.

Vegan Mushroom Wellington recipe

Number of servings: 8

Nutritional values per serving:

Calories – 554, Fat – 37 g, Carbohydrate – 47 g, Fiber – NA, Protein – 10.9 g

Ingredients:

- 8 large Portobello mushrooms, discard stems, cleaned
- 6 tablespoons olive oil
- 8 sprigs thyme, leaves picked
- 2 tablespoons Dijon mustard
- 6 large onions, peeled, chopped
- 21 ounces baby spinach
- 2 sheets vegan puff pastry
- Salt to taste
- Pepper to taste

For vegan egg wash:

- 2 tablespoons aquafaba
- 2 teaspoons oil
- 2 tablespoons almond milk or cashew milk
- 1 teaspoon maple syrup or brown rice syrup

Directions:

1. Place a pan over medium-low heat. Add 2 tablespoons oil. When the oil is heated, add onion, salt, and pepper and stir.
2. Lower the heat and cook until golden brown. Stir occasionally.
3. Take out the onions from the pan and place on a plate lined with paper towels.
4. Add spinach into the same pan and cook until it wilts.
5. Raise the heat to medium-high heat. Add 4 tablespoons oil. When the oil is heated, add mushrooms, with the stem side facing up. When the underside is golden brown, flip sides. Cook the other side until golden brown.

6. Remove with a slotted spoon and place on a plate lined with paper towels.
7. When it cools, transfer into a bowl and chill for an hour.
8. Line a large baking sheet with parchment paper.
9. Place the pastry sheets, on your countertop.
10. Spread ½ the onions among the 2 pastry sheets, on the center third of the sheets, leaving a border of ¾ inch on the edges of the sheets.
11. Spread half the spinach over the onions. Spoon the Dijon mustard over the mushrooms and sprinkle salt and pepper. Place 4 mushrooms on each sheet, over the spinach.
12. Sprinkle thyme and spread the remaining spinach and finally onions.
13. Fold one side of the pastry over the filling and roll the pastry and place it on the baking sheet with the seam side facing down. Press the edges together to seal well.
14. To make the vegan egg wash: Mix together all the ingredients for a vegan egg wash in a bowl.
15. Brush the pastry with this mixture, lightly. Freeze for 10 minutes.
16. Repeat the previous step once more.
17. Bake in a preheated oven at 350º F for about 30 minutes or until golden brown.

Vegan "Chicken" Parmesan

Number of servings: 8

Nutritional values per serving: Without pasta

Calories – 577, Fat – 21.6 g, Carbohydrate – 83.5 g, Fiber – 13.7 g, Protein – 13.3 g

Ingredients:

For cutlets:

- 2 cans (14 ounces each) chickpeas, drained, rinsed
- ½ cup chickpea flour
- 6 cloves garlic, peeled, minced
- 4 tablespoons plain soymilk or almond milk

- 2 tablespoons lemon juice
- 1 cup cornmeal
- 2 small onions, quartered
- ¼ cup chopped fresh parsley
- 2 tablespoons ground flaxseeds
- Salt to taste
- Pepper to taste

For batter:

- 1 cup plain soy milk or almond milk
- 4 tablespoons ground flax seeds
- ½ cup cornstarch

For cornmeal coating:

- 1 cup cornmeal
- ½ teaspoon salt
- 2 teaspoons Italian seasoning blend
- ½ teaspoon pepper

To fry:

- ½ cup olive oil

To serve:

- 4-6 cups marinara sauce
- Hot cooked pasta
- Cashew Parmesan cheese, as required

Directions:

1. Add all the ingredients for chickpea cutlet into the food processor bowl. Process until finely chopped.
2. Remove into a bowl. Cover and chill for an hour.
3. Meanwhile, add all the ingredients for batter into a bowl and whisk well. Let it rest for about 20 minutes.

4. Add all the ingredients for cornmeal coating into a bowl and stir.
5. Remove the chickpea mixture from the refrigerator and divide into 8 equal portions. Shape into an oval shape of about 5 inches in length and 3 inches in width.
6. Place a large nonstick pan over medium heat. Add some oil and swirl the pan to spread the oil. Be generous with the oil.
7. First, dip a cutlet in the batter. Shake to drop off excess batter. Next dredge in cornmeal mixture and place in the pan.
8. Repeat the previous step and place as many cutlets as possible. Cook until the underside is golden brown. Flip sides and cook the other side until golden brown.
9. Remove with a slotted spoon and place on a plate lined with paper towels.
10. Cook the remaining in batches.
11. Spoon marinara sauce over the cutlets. Sprinkle vegan Parmesan cheese on top and serve.

Tip: Refer recipe Zucchini gratin in Chapter six: Vegan casserole Recipes, for homemade vegan Parmesan cheese.

Chapter Fifteen: Vegan Sweet Meal Recipes

Bored with having savory meals? Try these recipes for that occasional sweet craving that is filling as well.

Tip: I sometimes make pancake casserole for dinner. Make about 8-10 pancakes and some vegan custard. Slice some bananas and chop some nuts. Spread the custard on the bottom of a baking dish and place a layer of pancakes. Spread a layer of fruit and nuts. You can also add chocolate chips. Spread some more custard and another layer of pancakes followed by banana and nuts. Bake it for about 25-30 minutes.

My kids just love this recipe and keep asking for more. You can use any of the pancake recipes that I have given in this chapter. You can make custard with custard powder following the instructions on the package. For chocolate pancakes, I make chocolate custard while for other pancakes I make a vanilla custard.

Sweet Potato Pancakes With Cinnamon Maple Sage Butter [Vegan]

Number of servings: 3

Nutritional values per serving:

Calories – 384.4, Fat – 38.6 g, Carbohydrate – 38.7 g, Fiber – NA, Protein – 7 g

Ingredients:

For pancakes:

- ¾ cup all-purpose flour
- ½ teaspoon salt
- ½ cup + 2 tablespoons mashed, cooked sweet potatoes
- ¾ cup soymilk

- 1 ¾ teaspoons baking powder
- ¼ teaspoon ground nutmeg
- 1 egg replacer, beaten
- 2 tablespoons vegan butter, melted

For cinnamon maple sage butter:

- ¼ cup vegan butter
- ½ teaspoon ground cinnamon
- 1 tablespoon finely chopped fresh sage leaves
- 1 tablespoon maple syrup

Directions:

1. For pancakes: Add all the dry ingredients into a bowl and stir.
2. Whisk together rest of the ingredients into another bowl and whisk well. Pour into the bowl of dry ingredients and stir until well combined and free from lumps.
3. Let it sit for 5-6 minutes.
4. Meanwhile, make cinnamon maple sage butter as follows: Place a pan over medium heat. Add butter. When it melts, add sage and cook until light brown. Swirl the pan frequently.
5. Turn off the heat. Add cinnamon and maple syrup and stir.
6. To make pancakes: Place a nonstick pan over medium heat. Pour about 1/3 cup batter on it. Swirl the pan so that the batter spreads a little.
7. Cook until the underside is golden brown. Flip sides and cook the other side too.
8. Repeat the above 2 steps and make the remaining pancakes.
9. Drizzle cinnamon maple sage butter over the pancakes and serve.

Gluten-free Protein Pancakes

Number of servings: 4

Nutritional values per serving: 1 pancake without toppings

Calories – 220, Fat – 10.5 g, Carbohydrate – 15.5 g, Fiber – 11.5 g, Protein – 17 g

Ingredients:

- 2 scoops vegan protein powder
- 4 tablespoons psyllium husk powder, soaked in 1 cup water
- 2 tablespoons coconut oil
- 2 teaspoons baking powder
- ½ cup coconut flour
- 2 cups water
- 2 teaspoons vanilla extract

For toppings: Optional

- Maple syrup or agave nectar to serve, as required
- Toppings of your choice like berries, nuts, vegan sour cream etc.

Directions:

1. Mix together vanilla and coconut oil to the psyllium husk, which is soaked in water. Mix well and set aside for a while.
2. Mix together in a large bowl, protein powder, baking powder, and coconut flour.
3. Add water and mix well.
4. Add the psyllium mixture into the bowl of dry ingredients and mix until well combined.
5. Place a nonstick pan over medium heat. Pour about ¼ cup batter on it. Swirl the pan so that the batter spreads a little.
6. Cook until the underside is golden brown. Flip sides and cook the other side too.
7. Repeat the above 2 steps and make the pancakes.
8. Serve with maple syrup and toppings of your choice.

Tip: For chocolate pancakes, simply add 2-3 tablespoons cocoa powder to the batter. You may need to add a tablespoon or so of water.

Chapter Sixteen: Miscellaneous Recipes

Simple Vegan Omelet

Number of servings: 2

Nutritional values per serving:

Calories – 232, Fat – 7.8 g, Carbohydrate – 22 g, Fiber – 8 g, Protein – 22 g

Ingredients:

For the omelet:

- 1 ½ cups firm, silken tofu, drained, pat dried
- 4 large cloves garlic, minced
- Salt to taste
- Paprika to taste
- Pepper to taste
- 4 tablespoons hummus
- 4 tablespoons nutritional yeast
- 2 teaspoons cornstarch or arrowroot powder
- 1-2 tablespoons olive oil

For the filling:

- ½ cup onion, chopped
- 1 cup mushrooms, sliced
- 1 large tomato, chopped
- 2 cups spinach, chopped
- Salt to taste
- Pepper to taste
- 2 teaspoons olive oil

For topping:

- 2 tablespoons mixed fresh herbs of your choice, chopped
- 4 tablespoons vegan Parmesan cheese
- 2-4 tablespoons salsa

Directions:

1. For the omelet: Place an ovenproof, medium-size skillet over medium heat. Add ½ tablespoon oil. When the oil is heated, add garlic and sauté until light brown. Remove from heat and cool for a couple of minutes. Transfer into a blender.
2. Add rest of the ingredients of the omelet into a blender and blend until smooth. Add a little water if required while blending if the mixture is very thick and not pourable.
3. Transfer into a bowl and set aside.
4. To make the filling: Add oil into the skillet. Place the skillet back on medium heat. When the oil is heated, add onions and sauté until translucent. Add mushroom, tomato, salt, and pepper and sauté until tender.
5. Add spinach and cook until it wilts. Transfer into a bowl.
6. Place the skillet back on the heat. Add 1 tablespoon oil. Swirl the skillet so that it is well coated with the oil.
7. Pour half the omelet batter into the skillet. Spread the batter with a spatula or back of a serving spoon.
8. Take about 2 tablespoons of the filling and spread it all over the omelet.
9. Lower heat and cover with a lid. Cook until the edges begin to dry.
10. Remove from heat and transfer the skillet into a preheated oven.
11. Bake at 375° F for 10-15 minutes according to the way you like it cooked.
12. Take 1-2 tablespoons of the filling and place on one half of the omelet. Let it bake for a couple of minutes. Remove the skillet from the oven.
13. Place the toppings on it. Fold the other side of the omelet over the vegetables and serve.
14. Repeat steps 6 to 13 and make the other omelet.

Lentil & Bulgur Pilaf with Green & Yellow Squash

Number of servings: 3

Nutritional values per serving:

Calories – 259, Fat – 3 g, Carbohydrate – 42 g, Fiber – 13 g, Protein – 17 g

Ingredients:

- 2 ¼ cups low sodium vegetable broth
- 1 small onion, chopped
- ½ teaspoon salt, or to taste
- Freshly ground pepper, to taste
- 1 tablespoon lemon juice
- ½ small yellow squash, halved lengthwise and cut into 1/4-inch-thick slices
- ½ small zucchini, halved lengthwise, cut into 1/4-inch-thick slices
- ½ teaspoon freshly grated lemon zest
- ½ cup + 2 tablespoons brown lentils, rinsed
- 2 bay leaves
- ¼ teaspoon allspice powder
- 6 tablespoons coarse bulgur
- ½ tablespoon extra-virgin olive oil
- 2 cloves garlic, minced
- Fresh cilantro, or dill, chopped, to garnish
- Fresh parsley, chopped, to garnish

Directions:

1. Place a saucepan over medium heat. Add lentils, onions, bay leaves, salt, allspice, pepper, and broth. When it begins to boil, lower the heat. Cover the saucepan and simmer for 20 minutes.
2. Add bulgur. Cook until the lentils and bulgur is cooked and the broth is dried up. If you find that the lentils or bulgur is not cooked, add some more broth and cook.
3. Remove the bay leaves and discard it.
4. Add lemon juice and mix well.

5. Meanwhile, place a nonstick skillet over medium heat. Add oil. When the oil is heated, add zucchini, squash, garlic and lemon zest. Sauté for 4-5 minutes or until the vegetables are tender.
6. Add parsley, cilantro, salt, and pepper. Mix well. Transfer into the cooked bulgur saucepan. Mix well.
7. You can serve with pita bread.

Tip: I have a recipe for pita bread in my book Plant-based Lunch and Dinner recipes. You can check that out.

Couscous with Chickpeas, Fennel, and Citrus

Number of servings: 2

Nutritional values per serving:

Calories – 586, Fat – 16 g, Carbohydrate – 91.2 g, Fiber – 14.9 g, Protein – 22.3 g

Ingredients:

- 1 medium fennel bulb with fronds, trimmed, cut into ¼ inch wedges, set aside the fronds to garnish
- ¼ teaspoon ground coriander
- 5 kalamata olives, halved, pitted
- Juice of ½ orange
- Zest of ½ orange, grated
- Juice of ¼ lemon
- Zest of ¼ lemon
- 1 ½ tablespoons olive oil, divided
- ½ can (from a 15 ounces can) chickpeas, drained, rinsed
- ½ cup instant couscous
- Salt to taste

Directions:

1. Place a skillet over medium heat. Add 1 tablespoon oil. When the oil is heated, add fennel bulb and cook until golden brown. Stir occasionally.

2. Stir in chickpeas, lemon juice, coriander, and olives. Stir occasionally and cook for 3-4 minutes. Turn off the heat.
3. Add orange juice into a measuring cup. Pour enough water into the cup to measure up to ¾ cup and pour into a saucepan. Place over medium heat.
4. Add remaining oil salt, lemon zest and orange zest.
5. When it begins to boil, add couscous and cover with a lid. Turn off the heat. Let it sit covered for 5 minutes.
6. Fluff with a fork. Divide into 2 plates.
7. Divide the chickpea mixture and place over the couscous. Sprinkle fennel fronds on top and serve.

Tomato, Chive, and Chickpea Pancakes

Number of servings: 2

Nutritional values per serving: Without optional ingredients

Calories – 534, Fat – 10.5 g, Carbohydrate – 8.5 g, Fiber – NA, Protein – 42.5 g

Ingredients:

- 1 small onions finely grated
- 2 tablespoons semi-dried tomatoes
- ½ cup chickpea flour (also known as garbanzo flour or besan)
- 1/3 cup grated zucchini
- 3 tablespoons fresh chives, thinly sliced
- ½ teaspoon garlic powder or garlic paste
- ½ teaspoon ginger paste
- ½ teaspoon fine salt
- ¼ teaspoon freshly ground black pepper
- ¼ teaspoon baking powder (optional)
- A pinch red pepper flakes
- ½ cup water
- A handful fresh cilantro, chopped

- Cooking spray
- For serving: salsa, avocado, hummus, cashew cream (optional)

Directions:

1. Mix together in a bowl, chickpea flour, garlic powder, ginger paste, salt, pepper, baking powder, and red pepper flakes.
2. Add water and whisk well until smooth and free from lumps.
3. Add onions, chives, cilantro, and zucchini. Stir well.
4. Place a nonstick pan over medium heat. Spray with cooking spray.
5. Pour ½ the batter over the pan. Swirl the pan lightly to spread the batter. Cook for 5-6 minutes. Cook until the underside is golden brown, flip sides and cook the other side until golden brown,
6. Repeat steps 4-5 and make the other pancake with the remaining batter.
7. Serve with salsa, avocado or hummus or cashew cream.

Tip: If your batter is too runny, add a little chickpea flour, a tablespoon at a time and mix well each time. If it is dry, add water, a tablespoon at a time and mix well each time.

Chapter Seventeen: Side Dish Recipes

Baked Potatoes with Garlic and Rosemary

Number of servings: 3

Nutritional values per serving:

Calories – 179, Fat – 9 g, Carbohydrate – 23 g, Fiber – 2 g, Protein – 2 g

Ingredients:

- 2 tablespoons extra-virgin olive oil
- 2 cloves garlic, minced
- Pepper to taste
- 2 medium red potatoes, cut into ½ inch cubes
- ½ tablespoon fresh rosemary, chopped
- Salt to taste

Directions:

1. Add potatoes into a baking dish. Drizzle oil over it. Toss well. Sprinkle salt, pepper, garlic, and rosemary and toss well.
2. Bake in a preheated oven at 350° F for about 30 minutes or until cooked and golden brown.

Tip: You can drizzle some vegan sour cream on top and serve. You can also sprinkle some vegan cheese.

Marinated Mushroom and Eggplant with Peanut Sauce

Number of servings: 8

Nutritional values per serving:

Calories – 807, Fat – 68.7 g, Carbohydrate – 38 g, Fiber – 16.8 g, Protein – 23.1 g

Ingredients:

For vegetables

- 4 medium eggplants cut into 1 inch cubes
- 1 pound crimini mushrooms, stems discarded, halved

For marinade:

- 2 teaspoons ground cumin
- 2 tablespoons grated ginger
- 8 tablespoons soy sauce
- 2 teaspoons ground coriander
- 2 tablespoons lemon juice
- 4 cloves garlic, crushed
- 1 cup sunflower oil

For peanut sauce:

- 2 cups crunchy peanut butter
- 1 teaspoon coriander seeds
- 1 teaspoon cumin seeds
- 3 cloves garlic, minced
- ¼ cup chopped onion
- 1 teaspoon salt to taste
- 1 cup coconut milk
- 2 cups water
- 2 tablespoons lemon juice
- ½ teaspoon chili powder

Directions:

1. Insert eggplant pieces and mushrooms onto metal skewers. Place the skewers in a wide shallow dish.
2. For the marinade: Add coriander, cumin, garlic and ginger into a skillet. Place the skillet over high heat. Stir-fry for a minute or so until aromatic. Turn off the heat.

3. Add soy sauce, lemon juice, and oil. Whisk well and pour over the skewers. Let it marinate for 30 minutes.
4. Meanwhile, make the peanut sauce as follows: Add garlic, coriander and cumin seeds into the small blender jar and blend until smooth.
5. Transfer into a pan. Add rest of the ingredients for peanut butter. Place the pan over medium heat. Stir frequently until thick. Pour into a bowl.
6. Remove the skewers from the marinade and grill on a preheated grill until tender. Turn the skewers a few times while grilling.
7. Serve with peanut sauce.

Tip: You can try replacing the peanut sauce with Thai peanut sauce in Chapter three: Vegan Sauce Recipes.

Grilled Brussels sprouts with Balsamic Glaze

Number of servings: 2

Nutritional values per serving:

Calories – 118, Fat – 7 g, Carbohydrate – 12.5 g, Fiber – 4.5 g, Protein – 4 g

Ingredients:

- ½ pound Brussels sprouts, trimmed, halved
- Salt to taste
- Freshly cracked black pepper
- 1 tablespoon olive oil
- 2 teaspoons balsamic glaze

Directions:

1. Place a large sheet of foil on your countertop. Thread the Brussels sprouts on to the skewers. Place on the foil. Sprinkle oil, salt, and pepper. Cover the skewers along with Brussels sprouts with foil.
2. Preheat a grill. Lower the temperature to low and place the foil packet on the grill. Cook for about 30 minutes. Turn the foil around every 5-6 minutes.

3. When done, uncover, drizzle balsamic glaze over the Brussels sprouts and serve.

Izakaya style Japanese Soybeans in a Pod (Edamame)

Number of servings:

Nutritional values per serving:

Calories – 124.1, Fat – 5.5 g, Carbohydrate – 9.3 g, Fiber – 3.2 g, Protein – 10.5 g

Ingredients:

- ½ pound edamame with pods
- ¼ teaspoon salt
- ½ tablespoon sake
- 1 clove garlic, minced
- 3 cups water
- 1 tablespoon soy sauce
- ½ tablespoon mirin
- ½ teaspoon sesame oil
- Hot chili paste (optional)
- Salt to taste

Directions:

1. Pour water in a saucepan and add ¼ teaspoon salt. When it begins to boil, add edamame. Cover the saucepan and cook for 5-6 minutes until tender.
2. Drain the soybeans and rinse in cold water.
3. To the same saucepan add 3 tablespoons water, soy sauce, sake, mirin, garlic, and edamame. Cook over medium heat until the liquid in the pan is reduced to around two thirds the original quantity. Stir frequently. Add hot chili paste if using.
4. Slowly add the sesame oil and mix well. Season with salt and serve.

Tip: You can replace edamame with sugar snap peas

Herbed Corn & Edamame Succotash

Number of servings: 3

Nutritional values per serving:

Calories – 111, Fat – 4 g, Carbohydrate – 14 g, Fiber – 3 g, Protein – 5 g

Ingredients:

- ¾ cup fresh or frozen shelled edamame
- ¼ cup chopped red bell pepper,
- 1 clove garlic, minced
- ½ tablespoon canola oil
- ½ small onion, chopped
- 1 cup frozen corn kernels, thawed
- A handful fresh basil chopped or ½ teaspoon dried basil
- A handful fresh parsley, chopped
- 1 ½ tablespoons dry white wine or water
- Freshly ground pepper to taste
- Salt to taste
- 1 tablespoon rice vinegar

Directions:

1. Add edamame into a saucepan. Cover with water. Add a little salt. Bring to a boil.
2. Cook for 4 minutes. Drain and set aside.
3. Place a nonstick skillet over medium heat. Add oil. When the oil is heated, add bell pepper, garlic, and onion and sauté until onions are translucent.
4. Add wine or water, corn, and the cooked edamame. Bring to a boil and cook for 2-3 minutes until dry.
5. Turn off the heat. Stir in herbs, vinegar, salt, and pepper and mix well.
6. Serve right away.

Stuffed Sweet Potato with Hummus Dressing

Number of servings: 2

Nutritional values per serving:

Calories – 472, Fat – 7 g, Carbohydrate – 85 g, Fiber – 22 g, Protein – 21 g

Ingredients:

- 2 large sweet potatoes, scrubbed
- 2 cups canned black beans, rinsed
- ¼ cup water
- 1 ½ cups chopped kale, discard hard ribs and stems
- ½ cup hummus

Directions:

1. Pierce the sweet potatoes with a fork, all over.
2. Place in a microwave and cook on high for 7-10 minutes or until tender. When cool enough to handle, split the sweet potatoes.
3. Meanwhile, add kale into a saucepan. Sprinkle some water and place saucepan over medium-high heat. Cook until kale wilts. Stir occasionally.
4. Stir in the beans. Sprinkle some water if necessary. Heat thoroughly.
5. Place a sweet potato on each serving plate. Divide the kale mixture and place over the sweet potato.
6. Add hummus and water into a bowl and whisk well.
7. Spoon over the kale mixture and serve.

Conclusion

As an athlete, it may sound like the vegan diet may not provide you the right nutrition. But I am sure after reading these recipes; you can very well debunk that myth.

Over the course of the book, I've given you a bunch of tasty and easy to cook recipes which will make sure that you get your share of protein and carbs. Remember that while being a meat free athlete ain't easy, this is hardly a reason to quit!

One of the greatest benefits of going vegan is the increased level of health you will experience and this manifests well beyond just your physique. Add to this the potent combination of healthy plant based protein and you have a winner! You can also choose to supplement with vegan protein powder.

Remember to prep your meals ahead of time for maximum convenience. I hope you've enjoyed the recipes in this book. Let me know what you think!

Made in the USA
Middletown, DE
21 April 2021